TWO DOZEN
FISHIN' HOLES

A Guide to Middle Tennessee

Two Dozen Fishin' Holes

A Guide to Middle Tennessee

Vernon Summerlin

Rutledge Hill Press
Nashville, Tennessee

Published in Nashville, Tennessee, by Rutledge Hill Press, 513 Third Avenue South, Nashville, Tennessee 37210

Typography by D&T/Bailey, Nashville, Tennessee
Maps by Tonya Pitkin Presley, Studio III Productions

Library of Congress Cataloging-in Publication Data

Summerlin, Vernon, 1943-
    Two dozen fishin' holes : a guide to middle Tennessee / Vernon
Summerlin.
      p.   cm.
    Includes bibliographical references and index.
    ISBN 1-55853-148-3 : $9.95
    1. Fishing—Tennessee—Guidebooks.   I. Title.   II. Title: 2 dozen
fishin' holes.
SH549.S86   1992   92-8001
799.1′2′09768—dc20   CIP

Printed in the United States of America
1 2 3 4 5 6 7 8–97 96 95 94 93 92

CONTENTS

Part Three • Stream Fishing

Part Four • Crappie Fishing

Appendixes

FOREWORD

I HAVEN'T HAD THE OPPORTUNITY OF SHARing a fishing boat yet with Vernon Summerlin, but I have read his informative fishing information concerning area lakes, rivers, and streams.

For the fishermen who are not informed as to where, how, and what to fish in the Middle Tennessee area, Vernon has compiled some very valuable information.

To my knowledge no one has written a book about fishing in Middle Tennessee the way Vernon has in this book. Not only does he tell you where to go, when to go, and how to get there, he adds other information that will prepare you for the fishing trip.

I look forward to fishing with Vernon soon.

—Jimmy Holt
"The Tennessee Outdoorsmen"

To Cathy

The love of my life
who shares and propels my dreams into reality,
gives her time, heart, and understanding,
and is truly my partner.

My wife.

Special Recognition

I USED TO READ THE ACKNOWLEDGMENTS IN books with little understanding of what those people meant to the author. Now I know that most of those books would not have been published without the acknowledged contributions. I want you to know that this book required the help of the following people to whom I owe a great debt of thanks. I applaud:

Cathy Summerlin, my wife, for being my editor, photographer, and fishing partner.

Georgia Summerlin, my mother, for giving me the love of words and the rules for their usage.

Doug Markham, Tennessee Wildlife Resources Agency (TWRA), Region II's information and education officer, for his valuable assistance and encouragement.

Doug Pelren and John Riddle, also of Tennessee Wildlife Resources Agency, for taking my calls and answering my many questions.

David Woodward, Preston Hulan, William Emerton, Doss Neal, Fredda Lee, Dayton Blair, Gene Austin, Harold Morgan, and Jim McClain for sharing their fishing tips, techniques, and honey holes.

Bill Hartlage, editor of *The Tennessee Sportsman*, for my start in outdoor writing.

U.S. Army Corps of Engineers for answering my questions and providing me with maps.

A special heartfelt thanks to two longtime fishing buddies and best friends: Bob Northcutt, who introduced me to canoe fishing, and David Orth, who introduced me to the fun and finesse of ultralight fishing.

Ron Pitkin, whom I owe a special debt of gratitude for believing in the idea for this book and patiently seeing it through, and the staff at Rutledge Hill Press.

I thank you all.

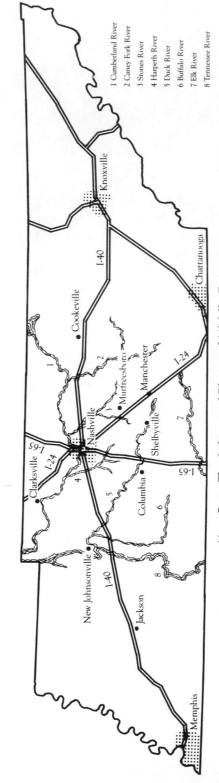

Map One: The Lakes and Rivers of Middle Tennessee

1 Cumberland River
2 Caney Fork River
3 Stones River
4 Harpeth River
5 Duck River
6 Buffalo River
7 Elk River
8 Tennessee River

Knoxville

I-40

Chattanooga

Cookeville

Murfreesboro

Manchester

Nashville

Shelbyville

I-24

Clarksville

I-65

Columbia

New Johnsonville

I-40

Jackson

Memphis

INTRODUCTION

It's been my pleasure to enjoy fishing in Middle Tennessee's lakes and streams for over twenty years. During those years I have spoken and fished with a great many anglers. Most shared their secrets for working various lures, methods of rigging baits, and how to locate honey holes. Now I want to share this information with you.

Since the purpose of this book is to help you catch fish, it answers the following questions: Where should you go fishing for specific species? Which baits should be used? When are the best times to go? How do you get there?

Sometimes you are given general information, especially for stream fishing, because streams are more delicate ecosystems than lakes and extra fishing pressure on a specific hot spot could destroy it. In the lakes and below the dams, I tell you where to drop a minnow for crappie, or I point out certain landmarks so you can locate my favorite honey holes for sauger, stripe, and other species.

This book is divided into four sections. The ten major lakes are first. After a general description of each lake, I describe how to catch the gamefish in that lake and where the fish are found with changing seasons. Spots suitable for bank fishing are listed. Finally, I give directions to marinas, launching ramps, campgrounds, and parks to make it easy for you to get to the lake and find nearby accommodations.

Part two describes the tailwaters below eight dams. Most of the tailwaters offer a smorgasbord of species in a small area. My favorite places are below Center Hill and Cheatham dams because they offer all the fish species available in Middle Tennessee except muskie. Center Hill's tailrace is an excellent place for fishing from a canoe.

11

My descriptions of the tailwaters include depths and structure, bank fishing conditions, honey holes for specific species, how to get there, and the locations of launching ramps.

Part three, the major streams of Middle Tennessee, is more varied. The format is not as standardized because streams have more distinct personalities. All of these streams are navigable, and I focus on canoeing, although a john boat will work. There are descriptions of access points and the fish species available in each stream.

Part four is a single chapter dedicated to crappie fishing. It is about a place called Big Bottoms that contains nine lakes with the best crappie fishing in Tennessee.

Because one species of fish will behave very much the same from one body of water to the next, you can get a bigger, more complete picture of a particular fish by reading about it wherever it occurs. For instance, some tips for smallmouth fishing in Dale Hollow Lake apply to that species in Center Hill Lake and the Stones River, and vice versa.

A fish's environment changes because of weather patterns, water conditions, and the seasons; and fish react to their environment in predictable ways. Learning a fish's seasonal patterns and reactions to its various living conditions will give you an edge. Appendix E lists publications to read for more information about fish behavior and fishing techniques. This knowledge will help you catch more fish under diverse conditions.

One of the quickest, surest ways to catch more fish is to hire a guide. Guides teach "how to" as well as "where to." This valuable information should stay with you long after you leave the water. Before you go fishing, make sure the guide knows you are going for an education. Catching fish should be secondary because you can go fishing more often than you will have the opportunity to learn from an expert. Appendix C lists the guides in Middle Tennessee. If you want to recommend some good guides I have missed, please send me their names and addresses.

Trout anglers will be interested in Appendix D: Middle Tennessee's stocked trout streams listed by county. Remember that trout travel and may inhabit other suitable tributaries. On the Buffalo River, for instance, unstocked streams have trout thanks to being near stocked streams.

Fishing pressure is expected to rise every year. This will bring about changes for us; we will have to share more responsibility for the survival of our sport. Fish are a renewable resource. The laws of Tennessee reflect a reasonable limit of fish for each angler to take from our waters and still leave a strong reproducing population.

Unfortunately, there are poachers. In talking with the many anglers and fishing guides who have helped me with this book, I heard of too many instances of poachers taking an unreasonable number of fish.

One example is illegal gill netting on the Caney Fork River. Fifty rockfish were netted in one night by poachers. Some of these fish weighed forty pounds and were over ten years old. The poachers bragged about it to someone, and that person did report the incident; but he refused to name names. The poachers have not been arrested.

It costs about a dollar a pound to stock our reservoirs. I resent poachers who take our fish to sell for personal profit. To stop them, call 1-800-255-TWRA to report poachers for both fish and wildlife. We are responsible for maintaining our sport, so let's do it.

With that said, you can do two things to make your fishing trips better. First, get a topographic map of the waters you are going to fish. Appendix A tells you where and how to obtain these maps. They help you locate the channels, creek mouths, and other hot spots before you leave home. Once you find a productive area, make notes on the map for future reference. Your notes should include the season, weather conditions, the depth in which fish were taken, which bait you used, and anything else to help you on subsequent trips.

Second, but just as important, spend time talking to baitshop owners, anglers in the shop, and anglers at your fishing holes. They can direct you away from fishless areas and may tell you about a couple of their own honey holes. Striking up a conversation isn't easy for some of us, but it is usually pretty easy for two anglers to talk about fishing. When the shoe is on the other foot, be informative and helpful with anglers you meet. I have found that an exchange of information with an experienced angler leads to more fishing holes than either of us could fish in a dozen trips. It is also satisfying to help young anglers by sharing a technique and a productive fishing spot. They appreciate any information that helps them catch fish.

My friend William Emerton of Sparta gives inquiring anglers all the tips they could ask for on how to catch walleye in Center

Hill's Blue Hole. He still catches his limit, and he has helped hundreds of anglers by telling them what lures work, how to fish them, and where to fish.

With this book I'm striving to help you catch fish, as William does at Blue Hole. So let's go fishing.

Two Dozen Fishin' Holes

A Guide to Middle Tennessee

Franklin Guide Scott Morris pulled this wintertime smallie from Priest Lake.

PART ONE

LAKE FISHING

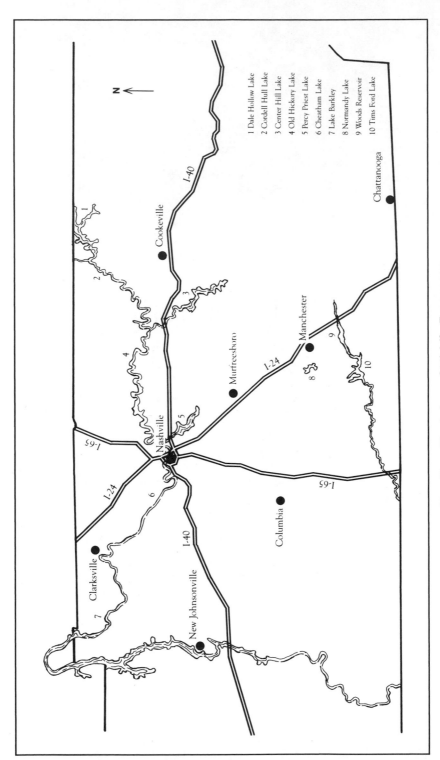

Map Two: The Lakes of Middle Tennessee

1 Dale Hollow Lake
2 Cordell Hull Lake
3 Center Hill Lake
4 Old Hickory Lake
5 Percy Priest Lake
6 Cheatham Lake
7 Lake Barkley
8 Normandy Lake
9 Woods Reservoir
10 Tims Ford Lake

THE LAKES

MIDDLE TENNESSEE IS BLESSED WITH PLENTY
of fishing holes. I focus on the lakes along the Cumberland River
and three lakes northeast of Chattanooga. Anglers in Chattanooga
and Knoxville are also close to some of these lakes, but all the lakes
are within a two-hour drive of Nashville.

The information provided in these ten lake chapters is more
comprehensive than in the other sections and should be considered
the foundation of this book.

Each lake chapter contains detailed directions to the water and
identifies the gamefish present; techniques used to catch each gamefish during each season; bank fishing conditions; location of marinas, docks, and launching ramps; camping areas; and some of the
local baitshops.

Now let's look at the ten big lakes in Middle Tennessee.

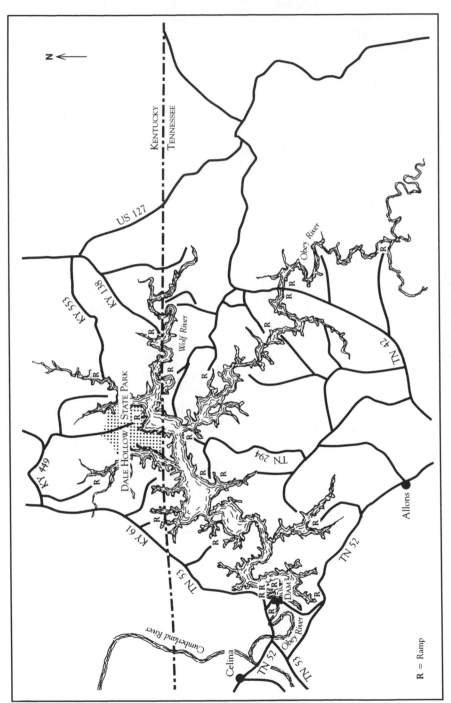

Map Three: Dale Hollow Lake

R = Ramp

CHAPTER ONE

DALE HOLLOW LAKE

DALE HOLLOW LAKE, HOME OF THE NEXT world record smallmouth bass, is halfway between Nashville and Knoxville on the Kentucky border.

Dale Hollow is considered a highland reservoir with flooded hollows and creeks. The upper end of the lake, where the east and west forks of the Obey River join near East Port Dock, downstream to Sunset Dock looks like a river.

Downstream from there the lake begins to widen. It has some steep bluffs but also has long shallow points that follow the contour of rolling farmland. After the Wolf River joins the Obey River, Dale Hollow takes on a lake's proportions.

The end closer to the dam is wide. It has steep banks, few tapering points, and high rock bluffs and is 150 feet deep. This depth provides the lake with cold water.

The cold water sustains species from the family *Salmonidae*—in Dale Hollow's case, rainbow trout and lake trout. Walleye represent the perch family and prefer cool water, which Dale Hollow supplies. The epilimnion, the upper layer of water, provides warm water for bream, crappie, catfish, largemouth bass, Kentucky or spotted bass, and world class smallmouth bass.

Dale Hollow gave up an 11-pound, 15-ounce smallmouth to David Hayes in July 13, 1955. This world record stands today. Gene Austin of Corporate Guide Service of Nashville, Tennessee, is sure he saw a fishing buddy lose a smallie pushing the fifteen-pound mark. He camped out in his boat for days trying to get it to hit again. Gene believes the new world record is still swimming in Dale Hollow Lake—just where, he won't say.

Today lake trout are near the twenty-pound range, and Gene holds the state record for lake trout, 16 pounds, 11 ounces, caught in May 1987. Lake trout, along with walleye, are gaining on the smallmouth's reputation.

Dale Hollow is largely in Tennessee, with several arms reaching into Kentucky. In 1991 a reciprocal agreement between the two states was revoked because of a difference in fish management methods. Although neither state has a clear-cut case for being right in its management, anglers lost their privilege to fish the lake with one license.

Now anglers must purchase a fishing license from both states to fish in each state's waters or be limited to fishing in the state where the license was purchased. Signs are posted on shore to mark the state borders.

Thirty-eight concrete boat ramps and fifteen docks give you a variety of put-in points on Dale Hollow's 61-mile length. Its 620 miles of shoreline ring its 30,990 surface acres. The fall draw-down averages about 12 feet, from summer pool elevation of 663 feet down to winter pool of 651 feet.

The Wolf River, which originates in Tennessee but meanders along the Tennessee–Kentucky border, and Tennessee's Obey River supply most of the water for the lake. Illwill Creek and Sulphur Creek are Kentucky's major tributaries. Tennessee has many feeder creeks with Mitchell, Irons, Ashburn, and Eagle being the largest.

Dale Hollow has been consistently found relatively free of sanitary and chemical impurities. The Corps of Engineers continues to ensure water quality as well as good fishing through its stocking programs.

The main highways leading north from I-40 to the area around Dale Hollow are, from east to west, TN 127 and TN 28 to Jamestown, TN 84 from Monterey to Livingston, TN 42 and TN 136 from Cookeville, TN 56 from Baxter, and TN 53 from the Gordonsville–Carthage exit.

GAMEFISH SPECIES

Muskie

The best months for hanging a muskie are from December into April. Most knowledgeable muskie anglers cast their lures between Mitchell Creek and Jouett Creek, and those who know a little more have narrowed the area, focusing on Irons Creek to Ashburn Creek.

Muskies hit large lures, up to twelve inches long. Big muskie baits are made by Storm, Rapala, Rat Man, and Bagley—many of the same lures you would use for big rockfish. Bucktail spinners from Mepp's, Lindy, and Bucher, and spoons from Dardevle, Hopkins, Eppinger, and Red Eye are also very good baits. Ambushing from the weeds, a vital part of muskie behavior, has earned them the nickname Water Wolf. Trolling the points is more profitable than casting. Big bait fish weighing close to a pound or about a foot long are appropriate for still fishing.

The limit on muskie is one per day with a thirty-inch minimum (check state regulations to be sure). The lake record is forty-three pounds, caught in Kentucky. The practice of catch and release flourishes among muskie anglers except when a true trophy is boated. They are not a fast growing species, and there are better tasting fish in Dale Hollow. The next fish is the best example.

Walleye

The best time to catch walleye is in contention. The U.S. Army Corps of Engineers' (USACE) *Fishing Guide* pamphlet states that December through March are the best months. Guides and dock managers say June through August are best. Both are correct because the fish are in different places for the months each mentions. Walleye are in the headwaters during the cold months and down in the lake during the warm months.

Whenever the best time is, the best spring fishing for walleye is in the Willow Grove and Pleasant Grove areas trolling a Hot 'n' Tot crankbait or Hot 'n' Tot Pygmy with a nightcrawler.

Walleye are fairly easy to catch if you can find them. During the cold months, beginning in November, walleye move to the headwaters in preparation for spawning, which usually occurs in March. They stay upstream in the big creek channels and rivers, moving into the shallows to feed and spawn.

After they spawn they slowly move down the lake during April and May. Their pattern is stable again for the summer months, following the large schools of alewives. Once you locate the baitfish, jig with curlytail jigs or live minnows below the baitfish. From sunset to dawn is the best time of day to catch walleyes.

Rainbow Trout

There are no bad months for catching rainbows. They are near the surface in early spring and fall because the water temperature is comfortable to them. The rest of the year you need to fish deep. Corn is the perennial favorite fished on the bottom. One-sixth-ounce Little Cleo spoons, and small Mepps and Rooster Tail spinners are the other top favorites.

Fishing at night near the dam during the summer is most productive. Rainbows are larger in the lake than below the dam, according to U.S. Fish and Wildlife Service officers at the dam. However, the state record comes from below the dam, a 14-pound, 8-ounce rainbow caught in December 1971 by Jack Rigney. (*See* Dale Hollow Dam, Center Hill Dam and Old Hickory Dam chapters for more about rainbow trout.)

Lake Trout

This cold water species was introduced into the lake in the mid-seventies. Anglers catch this fish year-round by trolling where the water temperature is between 50 and 60 degrees. In the summer that means keeping your lure near the one-hundred-foot depth. Down riggers have become the method of choice to reach this depth. Spoons are the lake trout's favorite lure.

Dale Hollow is the only lake in Middle Tennessee stocked with lake trout, but escapees have been caught in the midsection of Old Hickory Lake.

Smallmouth Bass

To catch Dale Hollow's darling bass, the bronzeback, you have to fish deep, fifteen to twenty-five feet to get their attention. Because the water is so clear, they reside deeper than in most lakes and may spawn as deep as eighteen feet.

Billy ("Mr. Smallmouth") Westmoreland of Celina says, "I would urge anyone who fishes Dale Hollow to use small lures and light line and to fish fifteen feet deep and deeper. Cloudy, windy days would be best because of the clear water. Concentrate on points, all points, for smallmouth.

"From mid-March until Memorial Day," he continues, "use

John Cates of Nashville has a love affair with smallmouth bass.

deep diving crankbaits, small grubs, and small jigs with pork. After Memorial Day, go to night fishing with spinnerbaits with pork and jigs with pork. Points and drop-offs are best."

Continue night fishing through the summer. "Mid-October is a good time for surface lures, until mid-November when the fish begin moving from deep water to winter areas, which are creek channel banks and drop-offs."

Billy's favorite time to catch smallies is from November until January with jigs and a lure called the Silver Buddy, which is made locally.

Trophy hunters concentrate on the midsection of Dale, from Mitchell Creek to the junction of the Wolf and the Obey rivers. This is a lot of water. To help you focus, look for these conditions: shale points that extend out from the bank about twenty to thirty feet and are close to a deep-water drop-off. Look for weeds and fish from fifteen feet down.

Gene Austin grew up on Dale and has guided on the lake since he was in high school. Gene says, "Look for pea gravel mixed with mud or red clay—that's a smallmouth place. In the spring, fish in front of willow bushes and on the secondary points up creeks."

Rather than trying to cover a lot of water and running out of gas in the process, get a map of the lake and choose five to seven creeks to fish. Focus on fishing a few places thoroughly. It will save you frustration as well as gas.

Catching a smallie is best accomplished with one-eighth-ounce jig head dressed in a chartreuse curlytail, or brown or black pork rind. Because of the lake's clear water, four- to six-pound test line is necessary.

Dale Hollow has another reputation to go with its smallmouth fame: it's a tough lake to fish. Do some homework before you go. Your best bet is to hire a guide for a day. At least call a dock in the area you plan to fish and get a report. Dock owners are very helpful and are informed on a day-to-day basis. Again, get a map, pick a few areas, and fish them thoroughly. Since Dale Hollow has plenty of smallies all over the lake, you need to fish deep and stay at it to be successful.

Don't forget that trolling works, too. You may catch walleye and muskie since they hang out in similar places to smallmouth.

Largemouth Bass

Yes, Dale Hollow has largemouth—some big ones—but you don't hear much about them.

The largemouth bass likes her (the big ones are female) water a bit warmer than her smallmouth cousin, and she is frequently found in the backs of creeks. Look for areas with a gentle slope and deep water nearby. The largemouth responds to the plastic worm or crawfish fished parallel to the shoreline. The upper end of Wolf River and the lower end of the lake, from Cedar Hill Dock up to Willow Grove Dock in the mouth of Irons Creek, are perhaps the best areas for Ms. Bucketmouth.

In the spring look for bedding largemouth in the backs of coves and creeks among sycamore and cottonwood tree roots. Angle for these fish with a topwater Rapala or floating red worm.

March to June are the months for daytime fishing. Night fishing under the willows during the summer months is a winning move. As with smallmouth, angling is good year-round for largemouth. July into September offers average quality fishing except during the day, but the quality of catches goes up at night using spinnerbaits and worms shallow on the points, flats, and backs of creeks.

Kentucky Bass

You can expect to catch the Kentucky bass, also called spotted bass or spot, in all the places you find its two cousins, the largemouth and smallmouth. The best baits are the ones you would use for largemouth bass.

Crappie

The best months for crappie are from March to early June and again from late September to early November. Dale Hollow does not have a strong crappie population. In the spring they will be in shallow water for their spawn, then move to deeper water around the drop-offs. Tight line fishing with minnows and small jigs works well in Dale Hollow.

Bream

The ubiquitous bream or sunfish. Worms and crickets catch these ever-popular fish around rocky bluffs on the main channel to the backwater of small creeks.

Rock bass, bluegill, and longear sunfish make up the largest portion of the bream in Dale Hollow. These three are easily found close to all the ramps and docks. You can find warmouth in the creeks where there are more downed trees and leaf debris.

Stripe

The Tennessee Wildlife Resources Agency stocked Dale Hollow with over 65,000 fingerlings in June of 1989. The fingerlings were freed at Willow Grove, Sunset, and Eagle Cove. These fish should be about ten inches long in two years and fourteen inches long in four years.

Fish in March and April in the headwaters with small spoons, spinners, and jigs to catch these determined fighters. The next best time is in the summer at night, fishing under lights along bluffs and at the dam.

Catfish

Channel cats seem to dominate the catfish population. They weigh up to fifty pounds and willingly eat stinkbaits, worms, and minnows. Channel cats like the bottom with stretches of rubble and gravel, and they prefer a little current. The good months to catch them are April to October.

Yellow or flathead cats differ from channel cats in that they do not like stinkbaits. They prefer crayfish and minnows and will hit your gob of nightcrawlers. Yellow cats lie deep in sluggish water among logs and other debris. Use your heavy gear for these cats; they grow to fifty pounds and can grow to one hundred pounds. The same months are good for catching yellow cats as for the channel cats.

BANK FISHING

You don't have to have a boat to fish Dale Hollow. Fish on foot above and below the dam and around the docks and boat launch sites. Shorelines in the mid to upper lake portions are also accessible on foot. A boat will give you the advantage of position to fish the steep drop-offs with less hanging up of your bait and lures.

Whether you have a boat or not, hiring a guide for a day is an excellent way to learn Dale Hollow. The guide provides all you need, including knowledge of the lake. It is his firsthand knowledge, not only of the lake but also of techniques and methods, that makes even a fishless trip worth the time and money spent.

FACILITIES

Docks and Marinas

Dale Hollow State Park and Dock, 6371 State Park Road, Bow, KY 42714-9728 (502-433-7431). Complete facilities—amphitheater, launching ramp, camping, RV hookups. From KY 61 in Kettle, take KY 449, turn south at sign. From Burnsville, take Cumberland Parkway to US 127 south to KY 90 west, then south on KY 449 and KY 1206; follow signs.

Cedar Hill Resort, Route 1, Box 85-B, Celina, TN 38551 (615-243-3201 or 1-800-872-8393). Bait, boat, bed/breakfast. TN 53 east from Celina; follow signs.

Dale Hollow Marina, Route 1, Box 79, Celina, TN 38551 (615-243-2211). Snack bar, all angler's needs except sleep accommodations. TN 53 east from Celina; follow signs.

Holly Creek Resort, Route 1, Box G, Celina, TN 38551 (615-243-2116). Snack bar, all angler's needs except sleep accommodations. TN 53 east from Celina to about 5 miles north of exit to Cedar Hill Resort; follow signs.

Hendricks Creek Dock, Burkesville, KY 42717 (502-433-7172) or PO

Mr. Whiskers is plentiful on the lakes of Middle Tennessee.

Box 35817-1, Canton, OH 44735 (216-854-4151 or 1-800-321-4000). Bait, boat, bed/breakfast. Two miles north of Kentucky–Tennessee state line on TN 53 or KY 61.

Sulphur Creek Marina and Campground, Kettle, KY (502-433-7272 or 502-433-7200). Snack bar, houseboat/boat rentals, RV hookups, cabins, groceries. KY 485 south from Kettle; follow signs.

Wisdom Dock, Albany, KY 42602 (606-387-5821). Snack bar, boat rentals, RV hookups, cabins, groceries. KY 553 west from Albany.

Wolf River Dock, Albany, KY 42602 (606-387-5841). Snack bar, boat rentals, RV hookups, cabins, groceries. KY 738 southwest from Albany.

Eagles Cove Marina, Route 1, Box 291, Byrdstown, TN 38549 (615-864-3456 or 1-800-346-2622). Snack bar, boat rentals, RV hookups, cabins, groceries. TN 325 west from Star Point; follow signs.

Star Point Resort, Route 1, Box 278, Byrdstown, TN 38549 (615-864-3115). Snack bar, boat rentals, RV hookups, cabins, groceries. TN 325 west from Star Point; follow signs.

Sunset Dock, Byrdstown, TN 38549 (615-864-3146). Bait, boat, bed and breakfast. TN 325 west from Star Point; follow signs.

East Port Dock, Star Route, Box 147, Alpine, TN 38543 (615-879-7511). Bait, boat, bed-and-breakfast. East from Livingston, north off TN 52 on East Port Road; follow signs.

Willow Grove Resort, Route 1, Allons, TN 38541 (615-823-6616).

Bait, boat, bed and breakfast. North of Livingston off TN 42, north on TN 294; follow signs.

Livingston Dock, Route 1, Allons, TN 38541 (615-823-6666). Snack bar, boat rentals, RV hookups, cabins, groceries. North of Allons, off TN 52 on Overton County Park Road; follow signs.

Horse Creek Resort, Route 3, Box 290, Celina, TN 38551 (615-243-2125 or 1-800-545-2595). Bait, boat, bed/breakfast. Between Celina and Allons, short distance north off TN 52 at sign.

USACE Launching Ramps, Camping, and Recreation Areas

Resource Manager: Franklin D. Massa, Route 1, Box 64, Celina, TN 38551-9708 (615-243-3136). Except Dale Hollow Dam and Obey River, write or call resource manager for information.

Dale Hollow Dam, Route 1, Box 64, Celina, TN 38551 (615-243-3554). Call resource manager for information on 42 primitive camping sites.

Pleasant Grove, 4 miles east of Celina on TN 5, near dam.

Willow Grove, northeast of Livingston, off TN 42, take TN 294 north.

Lillydale, northeast of Livingston, off TN 42, take TN 294 north, watch for right turn.

Cove Creek, north side of Obey River arm, 4 miles west of TN 42.

Obey River, Byrdstown, TN 38549 (615-864-6388). South side of Obey River arm, west of TN 42 near Sunset.

Other Camping Facilities

Rivertail Campground, Route 1, Celina, TN 38551 (615-243-2173). One mile east of Celina on TN 53.

Deep Valley Park, Route 1, Box 345, Allons, TN 38541 (615-823-6053). North of Livingston on TN 52 to Allons; follow signs.

Overton County Park, Route 1, Allons, TN 35841 (615-823-6666). On TN 52, 11 miles northwest of Livingston.

Standing Stone State Park, PO, Livingston, TN 38570 (615-823-6347). On TN 136 northwest of Livingston.

Eagles Cove Marina, Livingston Dock, Star Point, Sulphur Creek Marina, Wisdom Dock, Wolf River Dock, see Docks and Marinas.

Baitshops or Fishing Supplies

Rickman Shop Rite, Zion Hill Road (615-498-2606).

Knuckles Grocery, Allons (615-823-2239).

G&L Grocery, Start Point Road, Route 1, Byrdstown (615-864-6531).

Crouch's EXXON, Route 1, Byrdstown (615-864-3983).

West Side Market, TN 42 bypass in Livingston (615-882-2322).

Big Orange Tackle Box, north of Algood on TN 42 (615-498-9896).

CHAPTER TWO

CORDELL HULL LAKE

CORDELL HULL, FOR WHOM THIS LAKE IS named, was born near Byrdstown, Tennessee, and played an important role in American history. He was Franklin D. Roosevelt's secretary of state and was largely responsible for the creation of the United Nations. For these and other contributions to world peace, he received the Nobel Peace Prize in 1945.

Running between lofty hills and low, rolling farm land along its tributaries, Cordell Hull Lake is the most scenic run of Tennessee's Cumberland River. It is 72 miles long with 381 shoreline miles. At summer pool it has 11,960 surface acres with a depth of 87 feet near the dam.

The lake looks much the way the Cumberland River did before Cordell Hull Dam was built. You can easily see from one bank to the other. This continues downstream until some widening occurs east of Gainesboro between Trace Creek and Flynns Lick. The second section of the lake is a short run from Flynns Lick to Indian Creek near Granville Marina. The lower end is about a twenty-mile trip from Indian Creek to the dam. This lower end differs from the midsection, not so much in appearance but in warmer water temperatures and larger population of largemouth bass.

Dale Hollow Lake has a great influence on the water temperature of Cordell Hull Lake. While Dale Hollow Dam is generating and discharging the 47-degree water from the bottom of the lake, it can lower Cordell Hull Lake's temperature by 6 to 8 degrees overnight. Although this affects the main channel's temperature,

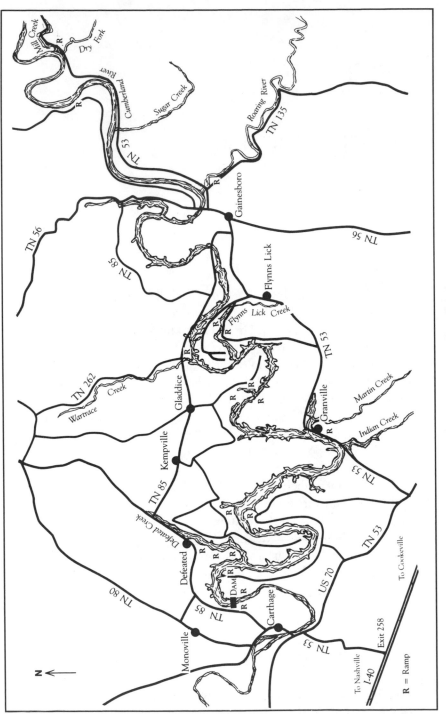

Map Four: Cordell Hull Lake

R = Ramp

there is little or no effect on the water temperature in the tributaries.

The lake has only two marinas, but there are twenty launching ramps, two immediately below the dam. From the dam upstream, the major tributaries are Defeated Creek, Indian Creek, Martin Creek, Flynns Lick, Wartrace Creek, Roaring River, Sugar Creek, Brimstone Creek, Dry Fork Creek, Mill Creek, and the Obey River.

GAMEFISH SPECIES

Smallmouth Bass

Joe Dick of Granville Marina reports anglers are catching more smallmouth than in previous years using crankbaits and jigs. Until recently the smallmouth has not been considered a significant contributor to the lake's gamefish population. That's changing.

The best catches were coming from Indian Creek under the trestle and up the right bank, from Martin Creek up the right arm next to the road, and creek mouths upstream from Martin Creek. A 5-pound, 2-ounce smallie was one of the biggest caught in this section of the lake.

Largemouth Bass

These bass are more frequently caught from the dam to Salt Lick Creek. The lake record is 9 pounds, 4 ounces. Two particularly good areas of the lake for bigmouth are Brooks Bend (or Phillips Bend on some maps) across from Hurricane Creek upstream to Flynns Branch (not Flynns Lick, which is farther upstream) and Salt Lick Creek.

Bigmouth are caught on the ever-popular worm and crankbaits such as the Mud Bug. This crankbait stirs up the bottom as it digs and bounces along the muddy flats and debris close to the river channel. Log jams on these flats are natural cover for bass, and the angler using twenty- to thirty-pound test line and worms rigged weedless can probe among the limbs.

Spinnerbaits are another good producer. Work spinnerbaits over the logs along the channel and the flats in the creeks.

May, June, and October are the best months in shallow water up the creeks. The bass are deep during the cold months.

Kentucky Bass

There is not a significant population of this bass in Cordell Hull Lake. Typically, you would fish for this bass in a smallmouth's habitat using largemouth worms, crankbait, and spinnerbaits.

Rockfish

Seventy-pound rockfish are caught below the dam and they run to forty pounds in the lake. The larger ones stay in the lower end near Defeated Creek and the smaller, seven- to eight-pounders move farther upstream near White's Bend.

The Red Fin has been the most effective lure, but the new ThunderStick has gained favor among topwater anglers. Both are topwater lures that imitate a fish in distress. All predatory fish, large and small, take advantage of disabled baitfish. An easy meal saves the predator energy. Rockfish feed on the surface early and late in the day. Working these lures with an erratic action increases their appearance of vulnerability and makes them more inviting.

Since Cordell Hull has cooler water in the main channel than most of Tennessee's lakes, rockfish aren't stressed by summer water temperatures and are more active near the surface during the summer.

Tennessee Wildlife Resources Agency stocks this lake, and the rockfish population is healthy and growing.

Stripe

Jigs, spinners, and spoons are the best lures for this fighter. Stripe will be found among the walleye and sauger from February through March, in the headwaters and mouths of tributaries.

They school and are caught in the jumps from July through September, with the latter being the more active period. You will find sauger mixed in with the stripe. This is unusual elsewhere but occurs on Cordell Hull.

Stripe, weighing one to two pounds, are usually found during the warm weather months in the jumps within a couple of miles in both directions from Hurricane Creek.

Walleye

Walleye don't get much fishing pressure, and they are abundant in this lake, especially from Granville to the Obey River.

Trolling is the most popular and most effective method for catching walleye, except during spawning season. Anglers troll spinner-nightcrawler rigs and crankbaits. In May walleye move down the lake and spend their days in channels, going to rocky bars and shallows at night to feed.

As the water cools in October, they begin moving upstream. Jigs and spoons hook them during their spawning runs beginning in November and climaxing in early April. The mouths of the larger tributaries are the most productive waters, including Martin Creek and the Roaring and Obey rivers.

Sauger

Sauger will mix with the walleye during the spawning runs and behave similarly. The main difference in catching sauger is that they feed on or very near the bottom, whereas walleye feed from the bottom up several feet.

Jigs and minnows, either together or separately, are the best baits year-round.

Bream

Crickets and worms catch bream all over the lake. Cordell Hull has a strong population of these willing biters.

Redeye (or rock bass) are also found in large numbers in Salt Lick Creek. They can be caught on crawfish, worms, minnows, small crankbaits, spoons, and spinners. They are usually found over a rock bottom in slow, clear water.

Catfish

Salt Lick Creek is a good place to catch yellow cats. Use nightcrawlers, minnows, or cut bait in the shallows at night or in the channel during the day among log jams and other debris.

Paddlefish

These "shovelnose catfish" are caught by snagging. The paddlefish is not a catfish but a member of the ancient fish family *Polyodontidae*. The fish is a filter feeder, swimming with its mouth open and filtering out plankton with its gill rakers. One of the two surviving species lives in the U.S.A. and the other in China. They are a source of caviar.

Snagging consists of ripping weighted treble hooks through the water with the aid of a stout rod and heavy line. Check Tennessee's fishing regulations for limit and legal snagging areas. Most waters have a limit of two paddlefish and no snagging within one hundred yards of a dam. A 104-pound paddlefish was caught near Gainesboro.

Crappie

Crappie are coming back stronger and bigger than ever. Reports have been good all over the lake. Fishing shallow water is best in the springtime. Look for stumps, stickups, brush, bushes, and log jams. Drop a minnow or small jig by the structure. They are in shallow water from March until June.

After June, look along the edges of creek channels as they go deeper for the summer months. They return to the shallows in late September and October to feed on schools of baitfish before going deep again for the winter.

BANK FISHING

Fishing from the bank varies with topography. Areas around launching ramps offer banks to fish. At Granville Marina a levee encircling the marina offers outstanding opportunities for bank angling. Five of the six USACE recreational areas offer bank fishing.

FACILITIES

Marinas

Defeated Creek Marina, PO Box 321, Carthage, TN 37030 (615-774-3131). Cabins, boat rentals, restaurant, fishing supplies.

Granville Marina, Granville, TN 38564 (615-653-4360). Camping, cabins, restaurant, boat rental, fishing supplies.

USACE Recreational Campgrounds and Boat Ramps

Resource Manager: Jackie Vide, Route 1, Box 62, Carthage, TN 37030-9710 (615-735-1034). Contact for information on USACE camping facilities.

Defeated Creek (615-774-3141). North on TN 53 at I-40 Gordonsville–Carthage exit, through Carthage on TN 263, east on TN 85; follow signs.

Roaring River. I-40 exit #280, north on TN 56 to Gainesboro, east on TN 53, right on TN 135; follow signs.

Salt Lick Creek (615-678-4718). South from TN 85 at Gladdice on Smiths Bend Road; follow signs.

Indian Creek. 6 miles southwest of Granville on TN 53; left on Indian Creek Road.

Launching Ramps

Damsite—west bank: TN 263 north through Carthage; follow signs.

Damsite—east bank: Just below dam. TN 53 east from Carthage, north on Horseshoe Bend Road; follow signs.

Carthage: 5 miles below dam in Carthage on north bank, just below TN 53 bridge.

Wartrace Creek: East from Gladdice on TN 85; follow signs.

Horseshoe Bend: East of Carthage off TN 53. *See* damsite above.

Sullivans Bend: See Horseshoe Bend.

Buffalo Creek: South from TN 85 at Kempville on Buffalo Road; follow signs.

Martins Creek: South of Granville on TN 96.

Smiths Bend: South from TN 85 at Gladdice and on Smith Bend Road to Salt Lick Creek.

Flynns Lick: On TN 53 northeast of Flynn's Lick.

Whites Bend: See Flynns Lick.

Brimstone Creek: TN 56 north of Gainesboro, east on Big Bottom Road.

Butlers Landing: On TN 53, north of Standing Stone State Park.

State Parks

Standing Stone State Park: See Dale Hollow Lake section.

Pickett State Park, Rock Creek Route, Box 174, Jamestown, TN 38556 (615-879-5821). US 127N north of Jamestown, turn northeast on TN 154.

Commercial Campground

Laurel Creek Campground, Rock Creek Route, Box 159, Jamestown, TN 38556 (615-879-7696). *See* Pickett State Park for directions.

County Park

Cumberland Bend Golf and Recreation Center, TN 56, Gainesboro, TN 38562 (615-268-0259). Boat ramp, restaurant.

Baitshops or Fishing Supplies

Mundy's, 4-Way Inn, Monoville (615-735-1815).

Outdoor Country, River Road in Gainesboro (615-268-2799).

Poor Boy's Tackle, Cookeville (615-528-5447).

Stan's Country Store, Route 3, Gainesboro (615-268-0881).

Joey's Sporting Goods, US 70S, Carthage (615-735-0813).

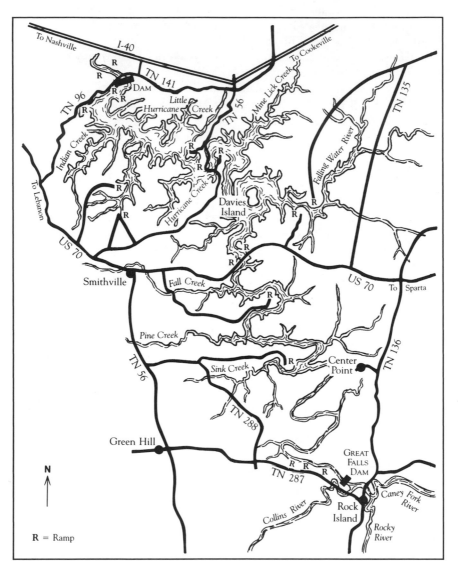

Map Five: Center Hill Lake

CHAPTER THREE
—————

CENTER HILL LAKE

CENTER HILL IS A VERY SCENIC LAKE. THE "Hill" is 64 miles long with 18,220 acres of surface area at summer pool and 415 miles of shoreline. The upper area of the lake has a depth of 37 feet and a depth over 150 feet near the dam.

The Hill is famous for its smallmouth bass, but the walleye is gaining on the smallie's reputation. Largemouth bass and spotted bass have very strong populations also. You can't beat the bream action in the summer on the Hill. Stripe and catfish are in excellent supply. In general, the Hill is a good fishery for most gamefish.

Recent years, however, have brought declines in the crappie and sauger populations. Tennessee Wildlife Resources Agency stocking programs for blacknose crappie will improve the catches in the next few years.

The upper end of this highland hill lake is riverlike from Great Falls Dam down to Davies Island, about two-thirds the length of the lake. Its feeder creeks do not have large areas of backwater but have deep channels. In early spring the upper end contains the spawning grounds for walleye and stripe. Smallies, largemouth, and spotted bass are caught with regularity along the Caney Fork River channel and in the feeder creeks.

The six miles to Big Hurricane Creek from Davies Island is the short midsection where the lake noticeably widens. Depending upon the creek size, the backwater may extend from two to five miles. Some anglers consider this area the "honey hole" of the lake. All prevalent gamefish species are here in abundance.

Big Hurricane Creek to the dam is the widest and deepest area with steep bluffs, points, humps, gravel bars, and larger areas of backwater in the creeks. This is the area to find summer walleye. Smallmouth, largemouth, and spotted bass are caught here with regularity, as are big bluegill.

There are eighteen launching ramps, seven marinas, nine recreational areas, and three state parks on the lake. There are numerous baitshop-markets around the lake from Rock Island Market at the upper end to Big Rock Market near the dam. The lake is only minutes away from Cookeville, Lebanon, Smithville, McMinnville, Sparta, and Carthage, and an hour east of Nashville via I-40.

Center Hill Lake is blessed with a great many feeder creeks. The main tributary is the Caney Fork River; other major streams are Sink Creek, Pine Creek, Fall Creek, Eagle Creek, Falling Water River, Hurricane Creek, Mine Lick Creek, Holmes Creek, and Indian Creek.

GAMEFISH SPECIES

Smallmouth Bass

Winter and spring are the two seasons to concentrate on catching your trophy smallie. In the winter they are most susceptible to the jig 'n' pig or jig and trailer. Cold weather fishing requires perseverance with a dose of patience. Bass are inactive and slow to react, and they are deep. Casting a one-fourth-ounce jig dressed in a Berkley's Power Craw is an excellent combination to meet these conditions. Because you are fishing in cold water for inactive bass, you must move your bait slowly and get it very close to the bass. The Power Craw leaks scent built into the plastic body (a combination of amino acids that smells like "breakfast cooking" to bass) to stimulate them to eat your bait. This may be the edge you need under these tough conditions.

Working slowly is the key for catching your trophy. Cast your jig or fish it vertically over fifteen- to thirty-foot-deep drop-offs. These drop-offs can be bluffs, points, or rocky banks. The following are some good spots to fish: Indian Creek at the junction of Jones Fork; Wildcat Hollow; Holmes Creek; Mulligan Hollow; Mine Lick Creek; The Narrows side of Davies Island and the north side of the island; and Eagle Creek. Once you learn these areas, look for similar places because these suggestions are by no means exhaustive.

Gene Austin of Nashville suggests marking the edge of drop-offs with buoys, then moving your boat back and casting to your buoys. In spring use slow-descending jigs, such as one-sixteenth-ounce on eight-pound test line or less.

Veteran anglers often use large creek minnows in the creek mouths from Davies Island downstream, including Holmes Creek, Eagle Creek, Mine Lick Creek, and Falling Water River. Angling with big creek minnows is sit-and-wait fishing. It takes more patience than jig fishing, but it pays off with bigger bass.

The size of your minnow determines the size of your hook—the bigger the minnow, the bigger the hook, the bigger the bass. Don't be afraid to choose an eight-inch minnow. First put on a half-ounce to a one-ounce slip sinker above a barrel swivel. Tie an eighteen-inch piece of line to the other end of the swivel and then to your 2/0 to 4/0 hook. Cast your offering down a bluff or steep point or along the channel ledge.

Make your cast into deep water, and once the sinker hits bottom take the slack out of your line and wait. If you put your rod down, open the bail or free the spool so the fish can take line without feeling undue resistance. Once your line starts swimming off, wait until you think the fish has the minnow well in its mouth or swallowed. Then try to break its neck setting your hook. You have a good deal of line out, and it has to cut some water before it becomes tight. A long, stiff rod helps for good hook-setting action. Its longer arc takes up more slack, and then it won't give when the line gets tight.

You won't be disappointed if it isn't a smallie on the other end—it will be a large largemouth, walleye, or catfish. The operative word is *large!*

As the water warms in the spring, tactics change to faster lures. Spinnerbaits and crankbaits are often thrown with great success. Jigs still work well, as do four- to six-inch worms. The water temperature in March moves into the 50-degree range, and smallies are in the mid to back sections of creeks. Bass are going to head for their spawning grounds when the water temperature reaches the lower 60s.

They nest on a gravel or rocky bottom away from silt near a log or big rock. Flippin' becomes an effective method for dropping these cover-tight bass. Dropping a worm or jig into their cover with the aid of a long Flippin' stick keeps you from getting too close to spook the bass but close enough to put dinner on the table.

Summer tactics aren't much different from winter tactics, except bass move farther and faster to take your bait. They are deep, down to thirty feet and sometimes more.

By June it's time to break out the night light for the most productive smallmouth fishing. Fishing deep drop-offs and steep points with jigs, worms, and spinnerbaits is the proven strategy.

Fall is another terrific time for bass. This is the time of year they school and feed in the "jumps" like stripe. They concentrate in the mouths of creeks and up in the creeks. Try the major tributaries mentioned earlier. Make long casts to avoid spooking them. Use an imitation shad. Spoons, topwater minnows, and spinners heavy enough to cast the distance are good choices.

Largemouth Bass

Center Hill Lake seems to have a homogeneous mixture of smallmouth and largemouth. That means you are as likely to catch one as the other. Both gamefish have strong, healthy populations in the lake. (Read the smallie section for where to fish.)

Largemouth like their water temperature a little warmer than the smallmouth. They will be a bit more shallow, and they spawn later than the smallie.

Use the worm more often for largemouth bass, but spinnerbaits, jigs, and crankbaits are also good choices.

Kentucky Bass

The spotted or Kentucky bass is smaller than its largemouth and smallmouth cousins, but it is just as willing to give you a fight. Some anglers claim it is the best fighter on a pound-for-pound basis. Spotted bass are scattered throughout the lake.

Gary Martin landed the Tennessee state record from the Hill in February 1989. It weighed 5 pounds, 8 ounces.

This is principally a river bass, so look for spots where there is moving water, headwaters, and feeder creeks. They lie in the lee of structure ready to attack prey. That prey can be your buzzbait—Countdown Rapala, Deep Wee-R, Rooster Tail, Zara Spook, or Pop-R.

Anglers have discovered that summer schools of spots will suspend over deep water. Your LCG (liquid chrystal graph), which

*William ("Wild Bill") Emerton of Sparta hoists
a limit of walleye from Center Hill Lake.*

will help you read the lake bottom, can assist you in locating these
strong fighters; then jig a spoon or jig among them. Watch your
line, as with most gamefish, they take the bait as it falls. When you
see your line twitch as you let the lure fall, set the hook.

Walleye

Center Hill has been proclaimed the premier walleye lake in
the state. Dale Hollow is a close rival, and either lake could have
the next state record. Center Hill once held the world record with a
twenty-two pounder.

Beginning at the famous "Blue Hole," a sixty-foot-deep hole
just below the Great Falls Dam, all the way to the dam you can find
keeper walleye. A keeper must measure sixteen inches.

My friend William ("Wild Bill") Emerton is the best walleye
angler in the state, although he rarely fishes anywhere other than

Blue Hole. He helps anglers with techniques and suggests where to fish. His helpfulness has made him a friend to many anglers there at Blue Hole.

William's technique is a two-jig rig. He ties one-eighth-ounce jigs with chartreuse hair about eighteen inches apart and fishes the swift current below the rapids below Great Falls Dam. He keeps the bottom jig on the bottom and drifts with the current. That's his early spring technique.

William changes his technique after the spawn. In May it's hard to find walleye because they are moving down the lake after their spawn. He switches to night fishing, casting a floating Rapala downstream and twitching it back.

Come June walleyes are found more easily along the main channel and near the mouths of the larger tributaries. Trolling is the most effective method from June until September or October.

Deep-diving crankbaits such as Arbogast Series 25 Mud Bug, Bomber Model 9A, or Mann's 30+ are required for trolling Center Hill's deep points, river ledges, humps, and other deep walleye hangouts.

Another successful trolling technique is the spinner-crawler rig. Tie on a Hot 'n' Tot Pygmy, a June Bug rig, or Hildebrant spinner with a 1/0 bronze hook; then thread a nightcrawler on as if you were putting on a plastic worm, leaving most of its length free to wave in the water. Slowly troll the humps, points, and bluffs. Sometimes walleye won't hit if you are trolling from the "wrong" direction. When you find a spot that should hold walleye or if you see them on your graph, try approaching the area from all directions. One of those directions should be right.

Crappie

Crappie is one of the top three gamefish in Tennessee. The drought of the eighties hurt the crappie's reproduction. Thanks to TWRA's stocking program and weather more conducive for reproduction, the Hill is showing a strong comeback. In 1991 TWRA stocked 360,000 crappie in the Hill.

Crappie don't languish in the shallows on Center Hill the way they do in most other waters. They seem to move into the shallows, get the job done, and get back to deep water. It probably has to do with the Hill's clear water. As you have read thus far, you have noticed fishing deep is the key to this lake.

After the crappie leave the shallows, you will need a graph to locate their cover, usually deadfalls. The banks are steep, and the tops of these deadfalls are deep enough to satisfy crappie. Here's how to catch them.

Once you have located a tree with its top down thirty feet or more, you are ready to see if any crappie are home. Simply tie a one-sixteenth-ounce jig, either with marabou or plastic curlytail, to four-pound test line and drop the jig vertically among the limbs.

Begin by imparting very little movement to the jig; if a breeze is rocking your boat, that is enough. If after a while you have no takers, give the jig a little more action. With your jig among the limbs, hanging up is likely, one of the reasons to start off with very little motion.

By summer the crappie will have moved nearer deep channels but near similar structures. The larger creek channels like Indian, Holmes, Hurricane, and Mine Lick creeks are good bets year-round. Use the same jig tactic year round also.

Bream

Big bream have their own army of anglers after them. These anglers shun the great bass, walleye, and stripe fishing for the cricket- and worm-loving bull bream.

As with all gamefish species in the Hill, fish deep. Summertime requires a heavy pinch of lead (or two) about six to ten inches above a number 6 or number 8 hook tied to four-pound test line. Slide on a red worm or a cricket and drop it to about thirty feet along a bluff wall.

If you don't get any action or if the bluegill is too small, move to a steep point and do it again. You don't have to wait long to know whether the bream are biting. Bream prefer the bait to move slowly rather than sit still or move fast.

Be prepared for another species to take your bait since all the fish are deep. This is especially true if you are fishing on the bottom for your bream.

The bream visit the shallows in the spring and fall and are easy to catch. Just about any cove or creek will supply you with a few hours of fun.

Stripe

The stripe bass is the only member of the white bass family in the Hill. But they are so prolific and such strong fighters you won't miss the others.

The heavy action takes place in the Blue Hole area from February until May. Stripe take one-eighth-ounce jigs bouncing off the bottom while drifting with the current. Bank anglers cast jigs, spinners, and spoons upstream, keeping a tight line and not retrieving the lure until after it is well downstream. This technique works for walleye as well.

Read the section on walleye because they are frequently found with stripe or at least in the same places.

From May until cold weather comes again, stripe roam the lake in schools. Summer fishing under lights is most productive. Trolling deep during the day along the bluffs and points with spoons, spinners, and jigs pays off, as does casting minnows deep and working them on the bottom at thirty feet.

Most anglers wait for the jumps, when schools of shad are being terrorized by a frenzied school of stripe. Fishing is frantic too! It's about as much fun as an angler can stand. The jumps occur more frequently in the late summer and early fall but are not limited to this time period.

Center Hill Lake has a hardy population of stripe and two-pounders are not uncommon. Ask at local boat docks or bait shops for reports of their recent action; they may put you right on them.

Catfish

Channel cats and flatheads or yellow cats are plentiful. These are warm-water-loving creatures and aren't very active in the winter. From spring to fall you should be able to load your stringer—a lot of cats or a big one. There are yellow cats in the Hill weighing seventy pounds, in which case a rope is appropriate.

Channel cats respond to stinkbaits and worms. Use large live minnows, creek minnows, or shad fished on the shallow bottom of coves and creeks at night for the giant yellow cats. By day fish the river channel or the deeper creek channels with the same baits. Anchor on a point at the junction of Indian, Holmes, Wolf, Little Hurricane, or Big Hurricane creeks and drop your offering into thirty-foot water.

BANK FISHING

Bank fishing ranges from excellent to impossible. Generally it is not an easy lake for bank anglers. The ramps, docks, and recreational areas are easy spots to reach. Getting to some of the bluffs and the steep points holding fish can be a difficult walk. When you are bank fishing in the headwaters at Blue Hole, you need agility to make it over the rocky bank, but it's usually worth it, especially in the spring when stripe and walleye are running.

FACILITIES

Marinas

Cookeville Marina, Route 1, Baxter, TN 38544 (615-858-4008). Restaurant, sleep accommodations, boat rental, fishing supplies. West of Cookeville, go south from I-40 at Baxter exit; follow signs.

Cove Hollow Marina, Route 1, Box 200, Lancaster, TN 38569 (615-548-4315). Full service, no restaurant. Buffalo Valley–Silver Point exit (#268) from I-40, south on TN 96 over Center Hill Dam, go 5 miles, left at sign.

Holmes Creek Marina, Smithville, TN 37166 (615-597-4387). Boat rental, cabins, restaurant. On US 70 go 3 miles west of Smithville, turn east; follow signs.

Hurricane Creek Marina, Route 2, Silver Point, TN 38582 (615-858-2211). Full service, camping, I-40 exit #273, go south on TN 56; follow signs.

Pates Ford Marina, Route 2, Box 78-D, Smithville, TN 37166 (615-597-4807). Full service, camping. TN 56 south of Smithville for 6 miles; east on TN 288 for 3 miles; turn left, go one-half mile; then right on Jefferson Road, go 6 miles; follow signs.

Sligo Marina, Hwy. 70, PO Box 300, Smithville, TN 37166 (615-597-5245). Full service, no camping. On US 70 south of Smithville.

Four Seasons Marina, Smithville, TN 37166 (615-597-7000). Boat rental, fishing supplies, ramp. US 70 east from Smithville, turn south on Evans Mill Road to Four Seasons Road; follow signs.

USACE Boat Campgrounds and Ramps

Resource Manager: Richard H. Puckett, Center Hill Lake, Route 1, Lancaster, TN 38569-9801 (615-858-3125 or 548-4521).

Long Branch (615-548-8002). Below the dam on west side.

Cove Hollow (615-548-8781). West of dam on TN 96.

Holmes Creek (615-597-7191). West on US 70 from Smithville; turn east at sign.

Floating Mill (615-858-4845). South on TN 56 at I-40 Baxter exit (#273); follow signs.

Hurricane Bridge (615-858-4164). *See* Floating Mill.

Ragland Bottom (615-597-7876). From Smithville 6 miles east on US 70, turn north at sign one-half mile past Sligo Bridge.

USACE Launching Ramps

Buffalo Valley: Below the dam on the east side.

Center Hill: Just west of the dam on the lake.

Johnson Chapel: See Ragland Bottom; turn 2 miles past Sligo Bridge.

State Parks

Edgar Evins State Park, Route 1, Silver Point, TN 38582 (615-858-2446 or 548-8135), overlooks lake. Boat ramps, docks, cabins, camping, trails. Buffalo Valley–Silver Point exit (#268) off I-40, TN 96 south to stop sign at Big Rock Market, then straight; follow signs.

Rock Island State Park, US 70S, Rock Island, TN 38581 (615-686-2471). Most scenic park on the lake. Bath house, camping, playgrounds, ramp. From McMinnville 6 miles east on US 70S to Rock Island; follow signs. Blue Hole section of Hill headwaters.

Burgess Falls State Natural Area, Route 6, Sparta, TN 38583 (615-432-5312). Scenic area, fishing, trails. On TN 135 south of Cookeville.

Commercial Campgrounds

Cumberland Caverns Park, Route 9, McMinnville, TN 37110 (615-668-4396). Go southeast on TN 8 for 8 miles; follow signs.

Monterey Bee Rock Campground, Route 1, Box 119A, Monterey, TN (615-839-9627). Hwy 70 exit from I-40 (#300), south to Bee Rock Road.

Hillcrest Market and Campground (615-761-3305).

Baitshops or Fishing Supplies

Poor Boy's Tackle, Cookeville (615-528-5447).

Big Rock Market, near the dam (615-858-9942).

Hayes Grocery, US 70W, Sparta (615-761-2288).

Cotten's Marina, Inc., Rock Island (615-686-2373).

Rock Island Market, Rock Island (615-686-2998 or 686-2007).

DeRossett Market, US 70, Sparta (615-935-2459).

Lewis Sporting Goods, Lantana Road, Crossville (615-484-3320).

DeKalb Market, US 70, Smithville (615-597-8424).

Center Hill Bait & Tackle Shop, 305 East Broad, Smithville (615-597-4811).

Ray's Crawler's, TN 304, Ten Mile, TN (615-334-5892).

CHAPTER FOUR

OLD HICKORY LAKE

IN 1960, IN THE UPPER REACHES OF OLD HICK-
ory Lake, Mabry Harper caught a twenty-five-pound walleye. Since
the transformation from Cumberland River to Old Hickory Lake,
the river walleye population has declined. Increasing numbers of
sauger, the walleye's cousin, have filled the niche.

Old Hickory has recently become known for its rockfish fishery, while largemouth bass are still the number one attraction. The
crappie fishery has grown since the drought of the eighties and
continues to get better.

Like all the lakes on the Cumberland, Old Hickory is a run-of-
the-river lake. Physically it is a river with its flow regulated by Old
Hickory Dam, and it is a more stable fishery year-round because of
the controlled flow. Usually there is no thermal stratification in the
main channel, but it may occur in its tributaries and embayments.

The cold water from Cumberland Dam and Dale Hollow Dam
keeps Cordell Hull cool. That cool water enters Old Hickory Lake
via Cordell Hull Dam, and cold water from the Caney Fork River
mixes in five miles downstream from the dam. This, along with the
fact that the water is frequently being used to generate electricity,
prevents stagnation.

Although the water in Old Hickory is well oxygenated, its
creeks and embayments can be drastically different. Water temperatures confined to these creeks and embayments can soar and
hold less oxygen. This can create a bonanza for anglers because fish
move from the creeks to the mouths for more comfortable living
and feeding conditions.

Map Six: Old Hickory Lake

R = Ramp

There are 97.3 river miles between Old Hickory Dam and Cordell Hull Dam. The lake has 440 miles of shoreline with 22,500 surface acres during summer pool and is about 70 feet deep near the dam.

The excellent stripe fishing is old news, but the new news, which many anglers are missing, is the rockfish population. Rockfish roam unbothered most of the year, and they are getting big. Rare catches of fish weighing forty to fifty-five pounds have been reported—rare because of the lack of fishing, not the lack of big fish.

Lake trout from Dale Hollow Lake have made their way into Old Hickory. Maybe this lake could stand a stocking of lakers.

Whatever reasons, anglers are enjoying a better fishery than a few years ago, and Old Hickory Lake is growing in popularity.

There are twelve USACE ramps on the lake, all between the dam and TN 109, south of Gallatin. Six of the lake's nine marinas have ramps. Many other ramps along the lake are seldom shown on maps (see appendix A for maps).

Fishing pressure has been light in past years but began to increase in the nineties. There may be two reasons for this. While nearby Priest has a fifteen-inch limit on its largemouth and smallmouth bass, Old Hickory does not and is attracting former Priest bass anglers. The other reason may be that the word is out about the lake's increasing largemouth bass population.

Beginning in the headwaters, the main tributaries to Old Hickory are the Caney Fork River and Round Lick, Dixon, Goose, Cedar, Spring, Bartons, Bledsoe, Spencer, Station Camp, Big Cedar, and Drakes creeks.

GAMEFISH SPECIES

Largemouth Bass

Old Hickory has become the new "glory hole" for largemouth fishing since the coontail milfoil took root. This aquatic weed is boon and bane. It has helped the bass fishing, but it has hurt other fisheries.

Milfoil has rooted itself from Shutes Branch to near Bull Creek. It forms mats where the water is five feet deep or less. The areas at the edge of these mats, where the bottom drops off, are ideal for largemouth bass.

Old Hickory also has piles of logs in the shallows and at the edge of the channel, stumps along the banks, flats with adjacent deep water, and creek mouth deltas that drop off into the main river channel. You can find bass in all these areas.

There isn't much wintertime fishing for bass on Old Hickory, but the few anglers who do brave the chilly weather catch bass, usually larger bass than are caught the rest of the year.

Springtime angling is hot. From March to May bass weighing six pounds are fairly common. Ten-pounders are not rare. All the major tributaries listed earlier become the hot spots.

The popular and productive lures are spinnerbaits, crankbaits, and worms. Deep-diving crankbaits, such as Rebel's Deep Wee-R, Poe's RC3, and Bagley's Diving B series, are favored for the spawning grounds. Crankbaits that bump bottom and stir up a little mud are the ones that get the bass's attention.

After the spawn, while the weeds are growing well, fishing Snag Proof's "Rats," the Moss Mouse and Boss Rat, will give you thrills bordering on a heart attack. Bass explode from under the milfoil chasing the rat as it scurries across the top of the mat. Work this bait fast initially; then slow it down if you haven't provoked a strike. The technique of casting it out so it "splats" on top of the mat and leaving it still for thirty seconds, then barely twitching it, leads to big bass blowups. Bass fishing doesn't get any more exciting.

As summer peaks, bass become susceptible to spinnerbaits and worms fished around the milfoil, docks, boat houses, log jams, and bars formed at the mouths of creeks. Flippin' is very productive also.

Don Denny of Watertown taught me to drop jigs and worms among the log jams, around the boat houses and milfoil on Old Hickory. He said he used to call it pitchin' but the pros got to calling it flippin', so it became flippin'. Don showed me how to swing the bait out to the structure and work the bait using my hand on the line instead of the reel handle. I finally caught my first bass, but he caught five while waiting for it to happen.

By August shad become the bass's primary target. This makes it more difficult for you to interest the bass with your offerings. Night fishing at the mouths of creeks and at the edge of flats with deep water nearby increases your chance of late-summer success.

Ole Bigmouth moves into the shallows for a final feeding frenzy in October. Casting spinnerbaits up in the creeks along the shallow banks should give you a lot of satisfaction. Come November, they begin to go deep for the winter.

Doug Pelren, fisheries biologist for Tennessee Wildlife Resources Agency, says the Florida strain of largemouth is present in Old Hickory. It was introduced accidentally or by "vigilante" anglers. This strain grows larger than our native northern strain.

Smallmouth

John Riddle, fisheries biologist for Tennessee Wildlife Resources Agency, says very few smallmouth are taken from the lake. There are some up the major tributaries in the upper end, but smallmouth are not plentiful.

Kentucky Bass

Dayton Blair, a guide from Mount Juliet, says to go after Kentucky bass the same way you would a largemouth, but concentrate your efforts in the lower end.

There is an increase in spotted bass in Old Hickory, says Pelren, and that shift is strong.

Rockfish

Old Hickory Lake is overlooked as a rockfish fishery except during the winter when anglers crowd around the Gallatin steam plant. The warm waters attract baitfish that attract the rockfish. Jigs, spoons, spinners, and crankbaits, as well as any lure that resembles a shad, take fish.

Rockfish swim unmolested most of the year. Occasionally, bass and stripe anglers catch some. It's from the lack of trying that more fifty-five pounders aren't caught. There are strong populations ranging from fifteen inches to twenty pounds.

John Riddle reports that Old Hickory has good forage and water temperatures for rockfish, and there are many in the lake in the forty-pound range.

They head up the major creeks and to the headwaters in the spring and roam the creek mouths at the river channel during warm weather. This is a fishery ready to happen.

Rockfish hybrids are already happening. The new lake record was caught March 28, 1991, by William A. Spain. It weighed 14.91 pounds.

Catfish

Nashville guide Harold Morgan says he can catch as many catfish as crappie while fishing with minnows. He takes cats from six to eight pounds near Cedar Creek.

From big yellow cats to the smaller blue and channel cats, Old Hickory has plenty. The best time to catch them is from spring to fall.

The Gallatin Steam Plant is an excellent place to fish when water is cool in the lake. The warm water discharged from the plant attracts all species of fish, including cats.

Shad, nightcrawlers, and minnows fished on the flats at night during warm weather will net you a barrel full of cats. The bigger cats are caught at night. Blue and channel cats take to stinkbaits very well, but the yellow cats prefer live bait.

During the day, cats are willing biters along the flats near deep water. The key is to fish where cats have access to a creek or river channel for an easy escape route. You can fish for them from a couple of feet deep on the flats and on the points of creek junctions down to the bottom of the creek, thirty feet deep or more.

If you like to catch cats, Old Hickory has them in abundance from one end to the other.

Crappie

Great in the spring! They swim fearlessly into the shallows each spring to reproduce and will fill your stringer. Crappie seem to spawn in less water on Old Hickory than on other lakes. You can catch them in five inches of water.

Using just about any tactic you want, from a cane pole to light spinning gear, from minnows to jigs, from a boat or the bank, you can catch crappie. Look in the coves. Along the banks of embayments, in just about any shallow place with a stickup or stump, you will find crappie.

Some anglers complain about the milfoil while others praise it for crappie fishing. The complaints are that the milfoil takes crappie from their former habitats that anglers have placed in shallow water.

Other anglers fish the weeds to catch crappie. Try dropping minnows at the edge or in holes with long fly rods or crappie poles. If there are no holes in the weeds, you can make some. Come back after twenty minutes and fish them. The weeds hold good concentrations of crappie during the spawn.

To avoid the milfoil, travel upstream beyond TN 109 bridge or downstream below Shutes Branch where it hadn't taken hold as of the summer of 1991. Fish the stumps, brush, logs, and boat docks to get your limit.

After the spring spawn ends in June, crappie slip off to the ledges of the creek channels. Use your graph to locate submerged logs or other crappie structure fifteen feet deep or more. Harold Morgan, a crappie guide from Nashville, says fishing Old Hickory is just like fishing Kentucky Lake because they have similar structure. So fish the creek and river channels, especially where there is something for the fish to gather around.

Bream

There are more than aplenty of bream in Old Hickory. Bluegill outnumber all other bream with the longear coming in second. Bluegills grow to one-half pound, but most are going to be half that size or less. They fight hard and taste good no matter how big they are. If they are big enough to bite, they are big enough to eat.

The milfoil is bluegill city. Drop a cricket or redworm along the edges and in the pockets and hang on. Away from the weed, fish along the banks next to logs, stumps, and rocks. During the summer you have to go deep along the bluffs to find the big boys.

Stripe

Stripe Alley is a term used for various sections of the lake, depending on the angler. The whole lake could be called "stripe alley." You can go anywhere and catch stripe.

They move to the headwaters and large embayments in February and March. During their spawn run, you can catch them drifting with the current near the bottom on jigs.

Come spring they move back toward the main channels and creek mouths. Some anglers say stripe are bigger from Spencer Creek downstream for seven miles. Others claim they are larger nearer the dams at either end of Old Hickory.

Old Hickory *is* stripe alley, all ninety-seven miles of it. Just go fishing—you'll find them sooner than you think.

Try the mouths of creeks and their points first. Next look in other stripe haunts. These include the steam plant channel, along the creek and the main channel edges, the downstream side of a point sloping into the river channel, or in the creeks and downstream sides of islands.

The most fun is fishing the jumps at the mouths of creeks

between July and October. Small spoons, spinners, crankbaits, and jigs are the lures of choice. Cedar Creek is almost a sure thing, but the same can be said of Spencer, Station Camp, and Drakes creeks. Also during these months cast close to the bank with a Shad Rap or Countdown Rapala. Stripe are not always deep when they aren't in the jumps.

When the water temperature reaches its winter temperature at the lower end of the lake, the discharge from the steam plant will be about 10 degrees higher. Anglers stack up like logs at a saw mill at the mouth of the discharge stream. Catches are made on Rooster Tails, Mepps spinners, Spots, or shad-shaped baits, Rapalas, and jigs. Just about everything works.

Although four- to six-pound test line is recommended, that may be broken by rockfish in these waters. Be prepared; carry some heavy gear with twenty-pound lines on a strong reel with a good drag system attached to a surf rod.

Walleye and Sauger

These fish are very similar in their physical appearance, choice of habitats, and seasonal movements. The sauger is smaller, reaching about three or four pounds, and has mottled coloring in addition to a spotted dorsal fin. The walleye weighs up to ten pounds, without a spotted dorsal fin but with a black spot at the base, and the lower lobe of its tail has a white tip. The two can mate and produce the saugeye.

When the lake's water turns cold, they move upstream and lie in deep channels until time to spawn. From the time they move upstream until after they spawn, you can have a ball. The catching can be furious on the coldest and most blustery days.

Sauger prefer to take their food from the bottom, and walleye will feed from the bottom and up a few feet. Jigs tipped with minnows are by far the best bait. Many anglers tie on a stinger hook to catch the short-strikers.

A stinger is a number 6 to number 10 treble hook tied with monofilament to the eye of the jig so it falls about four inches behind the jig's hook. This small hook goes through the tail of the minnow while the jig hook goes through the lips.

Jigs weighing one-fourth ounce and more are most commonly used. You need to have a jig heavy enough to hold bottom in the current and let you feel bottom as you work the jig up and down. Walleye and sauger bite so lightly that you barely feel the hit. Set the hook anytime there is any deflection; it costs you nothing and might pay off.

Heddon's Sonar, jigging spoons by Hopkins and Mann's, and a plain minnow are other baits that work well.

The areas below the dams are the hot spots during the winter until March or April. When the water starts to warm into the fifties, the fish start to spawn in shallow rocks or gravel. Night fishing is the most productive way to catch these fish in the shallows.

When the spawning is over, the fish move slowly down the lake. They go through a heavy feeding period in the shallows after they rest from the spawn; then they settle in deep pockets in the river channel. From June until the water turns cool, they are taken mostly by trolling (*see* Center Hill Lake—Walleyes).

Rainbow Trout

Most of you will be surprised to see this species listed. These are escapees from the Caney Fork River, which is heavily stocked with rainbow and brown trout. They make their way downstream, and several hundred are caught throughout Old Hickory each year. Probably every one is caught by accident except below Cordell Hull Dam (*see* Cordell Hull Tailwaters).

Rainbows eat everything from small insect larvae to crayfish and are not opposed to marshmallows sprinkled with garlic. They take small spinners and crankbaits. Other than below the headwaters dam and the mouth of the Caney Fork River you'll be lucky to find one (*see* the Caney Fork River section for trout).

BANK FISHING

Old Hickory is hospitable to bank anglers, especially closer to Nashville where the banks are less steep. The USACE recreation areas with boat ramps are good spots. Land is private to the water's edge, so get permission before you fish from someone's lawn. Don't overlook bridges and areas where roads run close to the lake and its feeder creeks (*see* Appendix A for maps that will help you locate these roads).

FACILITIES

Marinas

Anchor High Marina, 128 River Road, Hendersonville, TN 37075 (615-824-2175). Fishing supplies, private mooring.

Lakewood Marina, 2109 Lakeshore Drive, Old Hickory, TN 37138 (615-847-5408). Private mooring.

Old Hickory Marina, 2001 Riverside Drive, Old Hickory, TN 37138 (615-847-4022). Fishing supplies, ramp, restaurant.

Creekwood Marina, PO Box 315, Hendersonville, TN 37077 (615-824-7963). Fishing supplies, private mooring. On Saunders Ferry Road south of Hendersonville on Drakes Creek.

Drakes Creek Marina, 441 Sanders Ferry Road, Hendersonville, TN 37075 (615-822-3886). Fishing supplies, ramp, restaurant.

Cedar Creek Marina, Route 5, Mount Juliet, TN 37122 (615-758-5174). Boat rental, fishing supplies, ramp, restaurant. West of Hermitage, turn north of US 70N at the sign.

Gallatin Marina, 1198 Lock Four Road, Gallatin, TN 37066 (615-452-1515). Boat/motor rental, fishing supplies, ramp, restaurant. South of Gallatin on Lock Four Road on East Station Camp Creek.

Cherokee Resort, Route 5, Box 384, Lebanon, TN 37087 (615-452-1515 or 444-2783). Ramp, restaurant. South of Gallatin off TN 109—look for sign to turn east below the bridge. From I-40 take TN 109 north, look for sign to turn right.

Shady Grove Resort, Route 1, Box 222, Castalian Springs, TN 37031 (615-452-8010). Camping, fishing supplies, boat/motor rental, restaurant, ramp. On TN 25, go 7 miles east of Gallatin, south 2 miles on Harsh Lane; follow signs.

USACE Recreation Areas and Ramps

Resource Manager: William A. Payne, Old Hickory Lake, No. 5, Power Plant Road, Hendersonville, TN 37075-3465 (615-822-4846 or 847-2395).

Rockland, ramp only in Hendersonville.

Tailwaters South Bank, below the dam between Hendersonville and Old Hickory.

Lock Three, ramp only in Hendersonville.

Shutes Branch, 615-754-4847 for campsite reservations. Ramp.

Avondale, ramp. Southeast of Gallatin on US 31E. Turn right at sign.

Cages Bend, 615-824-4989 for campsite reservations. Ramp. South on Cages Bend Road off US 31E between Hendersonville and Gallatin.

Cedar Creek, 615-754-4947 for campsite reservations. Ramp. East of Hermitage on US 70N, turn north at sign.

Lone Branch, ramp. Farther east on US 70N than Cedar Creek, turn north on Benders Ferry Road and look for signs.

Nat Caldwell Park, ramp. At Station Camp Creek between Gallatin and Hendersonville on US 31E.

Gallatin, ramp. Lock Four Road south of Gallatin on East Station Camp Creek.

Martha Gallatin, ramp. *See* Cherokee Resort but on west side of TN 109.

Laguardo, north off I-40 on TN 109, past Spencer Creek Bridge on left. South of Gallatin on TN 109 at Spencer Creek.

State Parks

Bledsoe Creek State Park, Route 2, Box 60, Gallatin, TN 37066 (615-452-3706). Camping, ramp, bath house, nearby country store. Go 6 miles east of Gallatin on TN 25; follow signs south to lake.

Commercial Campgrounds

Yogi Bear's Jellystone Park, 1252 Hwy. 31W, Goodlettsville, TN 37027 (615-859-0348). Exit #98 off I-65, 1.5 miles north on US 31W.

Jellystone Park, Route 10, Box 300, Safari Camp Road, Lebanon, TN 37087 (615-449-5527). From I-40 south on TN 109 (exit #232) to south side frontage road, then east 2 miles.

Lakeshore Campground, 639 Walton Ferry Road, Hendersonville, TN 37075 (615-822-6638 or 868-2067). Camping, ramp on lake. From I-65, Two Mile Pkwy. exit to Gallatin Road into Hendersonville, right at #6 traffic light on Walton Ferry Road.

Baitshops or Fishing Supplies

The Bait Shop, Main Street in Hendersonville (615-822-7515)

Sport Marine, Lebanon (615-444-1880).

Fisherman's Headquarters, Saunders Ferry Road, Hendersonville (615-822-6809).

Flipper's Bait & Tackle, Hendersonville (615-824-5107); *Flipper's*, Pumping Station Road (also called Odom Bend Rd.), south of Gallatin (615-452-7719).

Smitty's Outdoors, Gallatin Road in Madison (615-868-3047).

Hunt's Sporting Goods, Hendersonville (615-824-1777).

Map Seven: J. Percy Priest Lake

CHAPTER FIVE

J. Percy Priest Lake

Priest is the most popular lake in middle Tennessee. It is a hill-land reservoir with river characteristics in the upper section, widening in the midsection and deep and wide near the dam. Priest has some highland reservoir aspects, including steep bluffs and drop-offs, sharp points, humps, and islands.

Priest Lake covers 14,200 surface acres during summer pool with 213 miles of shoreline around its 42-mile length. A depth of 100 feet is found near the dam. Fall drawdown usually begins in October, and a drop of seven feet is average. Full pool normally occurs in late April or early May.

The section from Fate Sanders Marina upstream is riverine. The headwaters consist of the two forks of the Stones River and Fall, Spring, and Stewart creeks. These creeks are the places to fish in early spring for crappie, black bass, white bass, and rockfish. From the mouth of any creek and downstream for several hundred yards are particularly good spots when the warmer creek waters enter the cool lake waters.

The midsection extends from Fate Sanders Marina to Hobson Pike Bridge. Priest widens and surrounds many islands in this area. These islands usually have steep drop-offs on one side and flat or gentle slopes on the other side. Fish, especially bass, tend to hold on the deep side in the summer and winter and on the shallow side in the spring and fall. Many guides consider the midsection the best, with the addition of Suggs and Hamilton creeks near the dam.

The lower section, from the bridge to the dam, has much the same topography as the midsection, with islands, humps, and coves, but the water is wider and deeper. Hamilton Creek and Suggs Creek are the main tributaries below the bridge. Both are excellent fisheries. Suggs Creek has earned its reputation as the most likely area to catch rockfish and hybrids.

Most lakes in Middle Tennessee are well known for one or two species. Priest rightly claims excellent fishing for crappie, large-mouth and smallmouth bass, rockfish, white bass, and the hybrid. Catfish would be among these if more anglers fished for them. This impressive list is due to the abundance of superb structure in the form of rocky bars, creek channels, humps, islands, ridges, coves, and flats and a strong base of forage or baitfish.

You are never far from one of twenty-two launching ramps on Priest. There are twenty USACE recreation areas, three commercial marinas, a county park, a state park, hiking trails, six campgrounds, and a wildlife management area.

Priest is ten miles east of downtown Nashville south of I-40. The other major access road is US 41 (Murfreesboro Road). All parts of the lake can be reached from these two routes.

Mount Juliet is as far east as you need to go on I-40 to access the eastern side of the lake. South on US 41 to Smyrna gains you access to the western side, including the east and west forks of the Stones River.

GAMEFISH SPECIES

Smallmouth Bass

Professional anglers like Tony Bean concentrate on the lower half of Priest for smallmouth. There is ideal structure for big small-ies, five pounds and more. Look for points with deep water access. Suggs Creek, Hamilton Creek, and the Stones River channels provide the deep water. When you find a point with a rocky bank leading away, spend time casting deep-diving crankbaits parallel to the bank and working a jig down its side.

Cook, Elm Hill, Seven Points, and Vivrett recreational areas, Long Hunter State Park, Hamilton Creek Park, rip-rap at the dam, and around the Hobson Pike Bridge are prime places to start your smallie search.

I talked with Gene Austin about fishing on windy days for smallmouth bass. He gave the following pointers that apply to other species also.

1. Fish windy banks because the wave action oxygenates the water. White caps or bubbles on the surface indicate air mixing with the water.
2. The wave action displaces crayfish, and they become easy prey for bass.
3. The wind pushes the water toward the shore and baitfish with it; more bass food.
4. The rough surface limits the fish's vision, causing it to feel safe. If it sees no danger, it behaves accordingly and moves into the shallows to feed.

Catches of smallmouth occur all over the lake, as do catches of largemouth; so don't be surprised if you hang a big smallie above Fate Sanders in the riverlike area. Seven-pound largemouths and smallmouths have been caught just up the channel from Elm Hill Marina.

Hurricane Creek flows by Four Corners Dock into a large bay and connects with the Stones River. There are several large islands above the Hobson Pike Bridge with good smallie spawning grounds. You can stay within two miles of Four Corners Dock and do as well as anywhere on the lake.

Use your graph or flasher to locate humps. These humps are found throughout the lake and come within five to ten feet of the surface. These submerged islands are also good spots to find smallmouth.

One last suggestion: the bluffs. Many species live along these bluffs among the cracks for protection or to ambush forage from larger cracks. Smallmouth fall into the latter category. A crawfish jig, jig 'n' pig, or a curlytail jig fished down the bluff can be productive.

From December until late February smallies are along the bluffs and channel ledges. Jigs are the ticket for these lethargic bass. Use a lightweight jig and a large trailer to slow its descent.

On Priest, the jig 'n' pig is giving way in popularity to the crawfish-jig and tube-jig. Berkley's Power Craw and Gitzit are two examples, respectively. In March and April crankbaits like the Deep Wee-R, Hellbender, and Rapala are killers, along with spinnerbaits, four-inch worms, and jigs.

Night fishing will be more rewarding from June through September in water from seven feet deep up to the bank. By October the water is cooler, and the bass are active for the last hurrah before winter. The frenzy continues into November. The Tiny Torpedo is a fun lure for the fall when fish school for their final feeding frenzy.

Largemouth Bass

This cousin to the smallmouth prefers a slightly different habitat: the stump- and brush-lined channels of the upper section of the lake above Fate Sanders Marina. Steep rocky banks give way to mud flats sloping into creek channels. Stones River and Fall, Spring, and Stewart creeks are the places to begin your bigmouth hunt. Worms, spinnerbaits, and crankbaits are favored.

From December until March, probe the ledges of the creek channels with slow, deep-working baits. When the water warms in March, work these same baits faster in shallow water.

After the largemouth spawns, usually in May, rely more on jigs and worms because bass will move into deeper water.

By June night fishing becomes the primary way to catch bass; and eight- to ten-inch worms are in order, as are fish scents. Berkley's Power Worm, Mister Twister's Phenom Worm (banana scent), and Culprit's Sticky Worm are winning anglers' confidence with their built-in scents and flavors. Built-in scents eliminate messing up your boat's carpet with the liquid spray types.

You can hardly beat October and November for largemouth fishing. Schools of bass are out to decimate the shad population. Catching them in the jumps can be the thrill you've dreamed of. Cast a shad-colored rattling bait like the Rattl'n Rapala, Rat-L-Trap, or Ratt'l Spot into the fray and hold on.

Like smallmouth, largemouth are found throughout the lake. Some of the largest have been caught within casting distance of Elm Hill Marina. It's hard to go wrong looking for bass on Priest.

Kentucky Bass

These smaller bass range throughout the lake. Fish for them much as you would for largemouth but look for them to be in areas more to the smallmouth's liking. This fish evolved in river systems, and it looks for current; in this respect it is like a smallmouth. It has a mouth more like a largemouth than a smallie, but its jaw doesn't extend behind the plane of its eye like the largemouth's.

Generally speaking, fish the lower end of the lake for spots. Up the river channel from Elm Hill Marina to Hamilton Creek has been productive for these spotted bass in recent years, as it has for its two larger cousins. You will also find spots in the headwaters.

Rockfish

Once the oceangoing striper was stocked in Tennessee's fresh waters, it quickly assumed the top bass position. It is a member of the "true bass" family, which includes the white bass, or stripe as it is called locally, and the brassy bass. It got the name *rockfish* because it prefers rocky waters. The term *striper* is beginning to replace the name *rockfish* because stripers have been caught for 300 years off the east coast, and the southeast is moving to that accepted name.

In the early 1970s it was discovered that immature rockfish will school in water around the 85-degree mark. As it matures, it seeks cooler and cooler water until it reaches the 68-degree range.

Topwater becomes the best place to put your lure during March, April, and May while the stripers are in the jumps. These jumps are rockfish and hybrids feeding on schools of shad near the surface. The rockfish's jumps are unmistakable; they will remind you of tens of crazed pigs wallowing in shallow water.

Most successful anglers cast large surface lures beyond the jumps and retrieve back through, if they have the composure to think about what they are doing. The popular Red Fin or a floating minnow by Rapala or Rebel will create a wake as it is pulled on the surface to attract the rockfish. A new lure that will take its share of rockfish is Storm's Jointed ThunderStick. It is a shallow-running, heavy-duty plug designed for long casts with a lot of swimming action. Rockfish will also take live bait including shiners, minnows, and shad.

In the warming waters of June you will have to find stripers with a graph instead of looking for them in the jumps, except early and late in the day. They suspend over deep water near the mouths of creeks and over points near deep water.

Anglers congregate early and late for surfacing rockfish during the summer on Suggs Creek between Seven Points and Long Hunter State Park. Drifting in the loop of the Suggs Creek channel at night using live bait pays off.

A split shot placed a foot to eighteen inches above a steel 3/0 hook is an effective way of drifting live bait about ten feet deep.

Give the big fish a chance to ingest the bait. They don't vacuum it in like a largemouth; they stun it and return for it or take it and mouth it before swallowing.

Another nighttime technique includes bumping bucktail jigs along the deep bottom, dunking live shad or big minnows, and casting to the shallows where the big fish feed. This activity should be carried out in areas known to hold fish during the day or where you can locate them with your graph or LCG.

From July into September you will find the fish in deep water where the temperature suits them. Locating them is the hard part; catching them is usually easy. During most summers a school concentrates near the channel about two miles from the southern entrance to Elm Hill Marina, above the dam along the old river channel. Jigging spoons or live bait brings them to the hook. Shad and shiners are the preferred live bait with bluegill taking third place. Remember the bigger fish are in cooler water—thirty or more feet deep.

There is a clique of anglers who cast chicken livers for rockfish. They begin an hour or two before dawn casting onto a shallow flat east of the dam. They sit and wait; then they stand up and fight. The rockfish are rather regular about feeding here.

Return to your springtime methods when the water cools in October.

Hybrids

This fish came from crossing the seagoing striper with its freshwater cousin, the stripe. This half-breed has a thicker body than the slim rockfish and retains the two tooth patches on its tongue inherited from its rockfish parent. This is a sure means of distinguishing a hybrid from a stripe.

Hybrids and rockfish have traveling habits too similar to distinguish. Where you find one, you are likely to find the other. You should fish for hybrids in the same manner you would for rockfish.

Many anglers and guides say that the hybrid gives a better fight than the rockfish on a pound-for-pound basis. The drawback is that hybrids do not grow nearly as large as rockfish.

Stripe

Stripe are the smallest of the three true bass in Priest. Look for them as you would for rockfish and hybrids, but not as deep. Stripe are easily caught in the jumps on spinners, spoons, and minnow lures. Live minnows crawled along the bottom take these fierce fighters.

Stripe school for a spring spawning run up the Stones River beginning in early March. After they spawn, they disperse down the lake until their summer reunion.

Like its rockfish cousin, it can travel twenty miles in a day. During the summer and into fall, they school and tend to spend a few days in one locale feeding on shad, their main food source.

When the water cools in November, they begin to move to the headwaters of the lake and to the larger tributaries, Suggs, Spring, and Fall creeks and the Stones River. They remain in the channels until the next spring.

Crappie

Harold Morgan has long been recognized as the king of Priest Lake crappie (*see* Appendix C for complete list of guides). His techniques are simple and effective. Harold selects hardwood dead-falls around the lake, about thirty feet long, and weighs down both ends by tying on concrete blocks with nylon rope. He deposits these crappie condos at various depths over the lake. That way some of the condos will have tenants year-round.

His crappie condos are approaching 200 in number. You can do the same if you spend a little time preparing to catch crappie. For springtime fishing, use a topographic map to locate drop-offs at the ten-foot mark near the mouths of creeks and coves. Place others between ten and twenty feet deep along creek and river channels for summer and winter angling. Put a few in areas where there is no crappie cover, such as barren flats along a creek channel. Make sure you mark your map where you placed them.

In January and February crappie are deep, between fifteen and twenty-five feet. In March to early April (depending on the weather) they move into the shallows where they will stay until May. During the spawn they may be a foot deep to nearly ten feet deep.

Spring, Fall, and Stewart creeks and the two forks of the Stones River are prime places. The midsection has its share also. Look in the shallows on the downstream side of the channel islands for spawning activity.

Cane poles, crappie poles, fly rods, and light spinning rods are popular with springtime crappie anglers. Using a long pole to drop a minnow among the limbs of downed trees and bank bushes takes the lion's share of crappie. Spinning rods with four-pound test line and small jigs take most of the others.

Jigs can range from one-thirty-second-ounce to one-eighth-ounce and be dressed in marabou, plastic curlytails, or live minnows—it's your choice. Use your preferred method; just about everything works during the spawn.

From late May until the next spring, crappie move down the lake. Morgan likes Suggs Creek for warm weather angling. Other anglers catch all they want just by moving deeper along the ledges and banks of the tributaries where they caught crappie during the spawn.

Water temperature determines how deep the crappie go to find comfortable living conditions. Look for water between 70 and 75 degrees. They will hang out on or near specific landmarks: stumps or condos on the river channel ledges or banks, mouths of coves, junctions of creek channels, outside bends in channels, and deep water around islands and around humps.

Harold has deep-water angling simplified. To use his method, tie a one-half-ounce sinker to the end of your line. About twelve to eighteen inches above the sinker tie a 2/0 gold wire hook; then tie another hook about two feet above the first one. Put minnows on your hooks and drop the rig vertically until you feel bottom.

He lightly bounces the sinker over the limbs on his condos. He uses twenty-pound test line to pull the wire hooks free rather than break his line. Pliers correct the bend in the hook if necessary.

Catfish

Channel cats show up most frequently in the Tennessee Wildlife Resources Agency surveys. They venture into shallow water where the netting and seining process takes place. The yellow or flathead cats like deeper water.

For a big thrill, go after the big cats lying on the bottom near the dam. Use heavy saltwater rigs and steel game hooks.

Yellow cats will take live bait in the form of shad, creek minnows, crayfish, and a handful of nightcrawlers. They bite best at night in the shallows and rest in deep water during the day on hard bottoms, preferably among logs and other debris.

Channel cats go for stinkbaits, worms, liver, and pieces of soap. They are caught in shallower water than the bigger yellow cats, and channel cats lie along the river channel's sandy or rocky bars.

Summer is the best time to catch cats since they are comfortable in 75- to 80-degree water. Look for them along the river channel on the shallow flats and on the humps at night at the lower end and midsection of Priest. At the upper end, look on and along shallow bars at night and down along the deep ledges during the day. Another good spot to look for cats is in the backs of coves among debris.

Bream

Worms or crickets and a cane pole are all you need to catch these sunfish. They reside close to the bank. During the summer when the water temperature reaches into the 80s, you will have to go deep to get the big ones. You can go to just about any place on the lake and catch all you want.

Fly rod anglers take good stringers in the spring and fall with popping bugs and terrestrials. Rocky bluffs over deep water is a prime target for these baits. During the spawn flip your offerings into the shallows.

Priest is home for bluegill, redear or shellcracker, pumpkinseed, redbreast, warmouth, rock bass, longear, and green sunfish. They range from next to the dam to the upper reaches of the headwaters.

BANK FISHING

Priest has excellent bank fishing from USACE areas, around the dam, near the marinas, and in many other places. Your choices are diverse on this lake.

You can reach most areas of the lake from nearby parking lots. Some of the best areas are where you can fish a point with a creek or river channel on one side and a shallow cove on the other. Elm Hill Recreation Area and Cook Recreation Area are examples.

FACILITIES

Marinas

Elm Hill Marina, 1240 Pleasant Hill Road, Nashville, TN 37214 (615-889-5363). Fishing supplies, restaurant, ramp. South off I-40 on Stewarts Ferry Pike; follow signs.

Four Corners Marina, 4027 Lavergne Couchville Pike, Antioch, TN

37013 (615-793-9523). Fishing supplies, restaurant, ramp. East off Murfreesboro Road (US 41) on Hobson Pike, then left on Hamilton Church Road; follow signs.

Fate Sanders Marina, PO Box 125, Smyrna, TN 37167 (615-459-6219). Motel, fishing supplies, ramp, restaurant. From Mount Juliet, take South Mount Juliet Road, turn left at Long Hunter State Park, right at Corinth Road, then left on Couchville Pike, right on Weakley Road; follow signs. From Murfreesboro Road (US 41), turn east on Sam Ridley Parkway, then left on Weakley Road; follow signs.

County and State Parks

The following have launching ramps:

Long Hunter State Park, PO Box 2968, Hermitage, TN 37067 (615-885-2422).

Hamilton Creek Park, 2901 Bell Road, Nashville, TN 37214 (615-862-8472).

USACE Recreation Campgrounds and Boat Ramps

Resource Manager: Roger Deitrick, 3737 Bell Road, Nashville, TN 37214-2260 (615-889-1975).

The following have launching ramps with camping as noted:

Cook Recreation Area: Camping reservations 615-889-1096. Follow signs on Old Hickory Boulevard, east of dam.

Seven Points Recreation Area, camping reservations 615-889-5198. Follow signs on Old Hickory Boulevard, east of dam.

Anderson Road Recreation Area, camping reservations 615-361-1980. Bell Road east off Murfreesboro Road (US 41) to Anderson Road or Smith Springs Road; follow signs.

Poole Knobs Recreation Area, camping reservations 615-459-6948. Take Fergus Road east off Murfreesboro Road (US 41) south of Lavergne; turn right on Jones Mill Road; follow signs.

Elm Hill Recreation Area, Stewarts Ferry Pike exit off I-40 east of Nashville; south on Bell Road; look for signs on left.

Vivrett Recreation Area, see Cook above.

Smith Springs Recreation Area, see Anderson above.

Hurricane Creek Recreation Area, east off Murfreesboro Road on Stones River Road in Lavergne; follow signs.

Fate Sanders Recreation Area, from Mount Juliet take South Mount Juliet Road, left at Long Hunter State Park, right at Corinth Road, then left on Couchville Pike, right on Weakley Road; follow signs. From Murfreesboro Road (US 41), turn east on Sam Ridley Parkway, then left on Weakley Road; follow signs.

Lamar Hill Recreation Area, see Fate Sanders above.

Stewart Creek Recreation Area, see Fate Sanders above.

Fall Creek Recreation Area, east off Murfreesboro Road (US 41) on Sam Ridley Parkway left on Gladeville Road, left on Mona Road; follow signs.

Jefferson Springs Recreation Area, east off Murfreesboro Road (US 41) on Sam Ridley Parkway, left on Gladeville Road, left on Mona Road; follow signs.

West Fork Recreation Area, south of Smyrna, turn off Murfreesboro Road (US 41) on Enon Springs Road; follow signs.

East Fork Recreation Area, south of Smyrna, turn east off Murfreesboro Road (US 41) on Sulphur Springs Road; left on Buckeye Bottom Road; follow signs.

Mona Recreation Area, see Jefferson Springs.

Four Corners Recreation Area, east off Murfreesboro Road (US 41) on Hobson Pike, then left on Hamilton Church Road; follow signs.

Gregory Mill Recreation Area, see West Fork above.

Nice's Mill Recreation Area, south of Smyrna, turn east off Murfreesboro Road (US 41) on Sulphur Springs Road; follow signs.

Damsite Recreation Area, visitor center, overlook.

Commercial Campgrounds

Nashville I-24 KOA, Route 2, Rocky Fork Road, Smyrna, TN 37167 (615-459-5818). From I-24W, take exit #70, keep right and take first left; go to signal; turn left.

Hermitage Landing, 1001 Bell Road, Hermitage, TN 37067 (615-889-7050). Membership resort park for RVs, tent camping, restaurant, cabins, bank fishing.

Baitshops or Fishing Supplies

Bill Clay's Sporting Goods, 2708 Franklin Pike, Nashville (615-269-3441).

Cumberland Transit, 2807-A West End Avenue, Nashville (615-321-4069).

Sports Unlimited, 5035 Harding Place, Nashville (615-331-1800).

Starkey's Bait & Tackle, 567 Stewarts Ferry Pike, Nashville (615-391-4460).

Tennessee Sportsman Unlimited, 4825 Trousdale Lane, Nashville (615-832-7393).

Friedman's, 2617 Nolensville Road, Nashville (615-244-1653); 2101 21st Avenue South, Nashville (615-297-3343); 2516 Gallatin Ave., Nashville (615-226-3279); 7069 US 70S, Bellevue (615-646-5305).

Nashville Rod & Gun Co., 73 White Bridge Road (615-365-3474).

Nort's Drive Inn, 1609 Murfreesboro Road, Nashville (615-361-1818).

Big Charlie's Bait Shop, Smyrna (615-459-9182).

Hooks and Arrows, Murfreesboro (615-890-7016).

Map Eight: Cheatham Lake

N ←

I-65

I-24

Nashville

R

TN 12

Old Hickory Blvd.

Cumberland River

I-40

R
R

R

TN 251

Ashland City

TN 49

TN 249

R
R
R
R
R

Sycamore Creek

Chapmansboro Road

R
R
R

Cheap Hill

TN 12

Cheatham Dam Road

R
R
R
R
R

Johnson Creek

Cheatham Dam

TN 49

Harpeth River

US 70

R = Ramp

CHAPTER SIX

CHEATHAM LAKE

CHEATHAM LAKE IS 67.5 MILES LONG WITH 7,450 surface acres and 320 miles of shoreline. This lake is not as deep as others on the Cumberland River, about fifty feet near the dam. This is a run-of-the-river lake, as are all the lakes on the Cumberland River.

Cheatham looks like a river until you get to the lower section. There is good fishing below Old Hickory Dam (*see* Old Hickory Tailwaters), but there are long stretches downstream that get almost no fishing pressure. The most popular and accessible fishing areas are close to Cheatham Dam.

Cheatham's main tributaries are the Stones River, Richland Creek, Harpeth River, Sycamore Creek, and Johnson Creek. Nashville is forty-two miles upstream from the dam, about two-thirds of the way from Cheatham Dam to Old Hickory Dam. It runs right through the city of Nashville. It is widest near the dam, and the best bass and crappie backwater is within six miles of the dam.

A closer look at this lower section reveals that six of the fourteen public launching ramps are within six miles of the dam. There are six more before you get to Nashville and only two above Nashville. There are two long stretches of river between ramps. From Cleeses Ferry in west Nashville to Shelby Park near downtown Nashville is about twenty miles and from Shelby Park to Old Hickory Dam is about twenty-five miles. There are places in these forty-plus miles that haven't seen a lure in years.

73

GAMEFISH SPECIES

Largemouth Bass

Bigmouth are the big attraction on Cheatham Lake. According to TWRA data compiled by Doug Pelren and others, conditions at Cheatham "indicate an overlooked bass fishery by anglers while relative weight values indicate good condition. Electrofishing samples show a large 1987 year class" and "a lack of fishing pressure has resulted in 24 percent of the largemouth fifteen inches and larger." These members of that 1987 year class should weigh close to three pounds now.

Forty-eight percent of the largemouth bass were from ten inches to fourteen inches long. Three percent were over twenty inches long and weighed over five pounds. That means trophy size bass are waiting for you now.

Let's compare Cheatham Lake to Percy Priest Lake. Largemouth bass in Cheatham that are fifteen inches or longer make up 24 percent of the population whereas Priest's fifteen-inch or longer bass make up 11 percent of population. There is a fifteen-inch minimum size limit on Priest but not on Cheatham. Also, Priest is one of the lakes getting the most fishing pressure while Cheatham is underused.

Preston Hulan of Nashville, who has fished Cheatham since before it became a lake, says, "It's a most challenging river—it's most unpredictable. There are no obvious changes, but something is different every day." His favorite bass holes are Johnson Creek, the submerged Lock A, Hudgens Slough, Dyce's Ditch, Sycamore Creek, the Ashland City bridge pilings, Marrowbone Creek, and Sams Creek.

Preston makes it clear you should "cast your baits parallel to shore and fish the mouths of the creeks. When you do that with a white willow leaf spinnerbait, you should be in 'hawg heaven.' But," he added, "if they don't hit that, throw a worm in the creeks around logs and such. If that doesn't work, throw a deep Wee-R, reddish color."

Preston says, "Spring bass will be close to the bank and at the creek mouths. Use a white spinnerbait in close, and retrieve it parallel to the bank." Later, bass will be moving out of the creeks back into the main river where they will maintain their territory until fall.

Largemouth rest where the current is quiet. Bass hold next to downed trees, rock piles, depressions in the river floor, the heads and tails of islands, or where current from another stream mixes with the main current causing an irregular bottom such as humps and bars. Bass wait in these places for food to flow past; then they swim out, take the food, and return to wait for another snack.

Big fish get the best ambush spots. Remove that lunker, and another big fish will move in. Better yet, let that lunker go back to her lair once you are through playing with her. To paraphrase the famous fly angler Lee Wulff, "A big bass is too valuable to be used only once."

Water temperature plays a very important role in bass behavior. Spring bass are shallow until late June. Largemouth bass find water temperature ideal between 68 and 78 degrees. Because Cheatham Dam operates its turbines for electric power and navigational demands, the river flow varies. The water is mixed, and the temperature won't vary from top to bottom. It will only change from season to season.

Doug Pelren's survey of the river in August showed no change in water temperature from the surface to thirty feet at the dam and only about four degrees from the surface to twelve feet in Johnson Creek.

Look closer at the lower end for good bass holes, and you will find the old submerged Lock A above the dam about a mile on the north side. It is between the shore and a green channel marker. Look for it with your depth finder. You are looking for a standing concrete wall that will make your depth finder jump from thirty-nine feet to four feet. Beside this wall is a good spot to jig for bass. The current will dictate the weight jig you will need. I've found one-fourth-ounce jigs to perform well under normal flow.

Johnson Creek is across the river and downstream from Lock A. You can go a mile or more up this stream for good bass angling. Upstream from Johnson Creek is the Pardue Pond Refuge and Pardue Recreation Area. This is prime bass backwater.

Dyce's Ditch is the first creek upstream on the same side as Lock A. It has a small opening but enlarges into bassy backwater. Don't go rip-roaring in there—it's loaded with stumps and flats and spring bass.

The mouth of the Harpeth River is upstream from Pardue. Dozier's restaurant is at the mouth, and you can park your boat at the dock there while you eat. It's the only place close by the river with this convenience. There is no ramp at Dozier's, but there is one about two miles up the Harpeth from the mouth at the Harpeth River Bridge on TN 49, southwest of Ashland City.

Across the river and upstream a mile from Dozier's is Sycamore Creek. The launching ramp is a couple of creek bends up from the mouth. Upstream from the launch, under the bridge and trestle to the right, is a slough. There is a quarter acre of fish attractors at the end of this slough. The water runs from six to eight feet deep.

Sycamore Creek is about seventeen feet deep from the ramp until you get near the mouth where it deepens to twenty-five feet. Then the bottom rises to nine feet and quickly falls to thirty feet in the Cumberland River channel. These water depths are relative, and the bottom shifts after heavy rains.

Upstream on the main channel from Sycamore Creek is Harpeth Island. Angling is good on the island's points and the south side where the current is slack. The south side of the island is the entrance into Hudgens Slough. Use your depth finder to locate dips and holes at the mouth.

There is an unnamed cut with about seventy yards of backwater down and across from Sycamore Creek, along the southeast end of Indian Town Bluff. It is the fishiest looking place to be so small. There is a stakebed inside the first bend. You may have to use a trolling motor to get in the mouth (watch for logs), but don't pass this water without giving your jig 'n' crawfish or white spinnerbait a workout.

All these creek mouths are good places to try, but consider the banks on the straight parts of the Cumberland. Stumps, fallen trees, and rock piles are common. So are submerged ledges and drop-offs, especially along the bluffs, but they occur on mud banks too. These are good ambush points for bass during the summer and winter months.

Most of the banks have shallow shelves that extend from three to ten feet before they drop to another shelf at about fifteen feet. The drop-off, depending on whether you are in a bend or on a straight part of the river, will slope from about 45 degrees to nearly 90 degrees. With your depth finder, you will see many irregular patterns at these drop-offs. These are frequently trees; some are covered with silt, and others have their branches free. Both are good places to jig. Use spinnerbaits and crankbaits to cover the water above the drop-offs.

Another aspect of bass behavior is that the bigger the fish, the less likely it is to school and the deeper it resides. Bass twelve inches or smaller will populate the shallows, taking their food from near the shoreline. They are easy targets for crankbaits and spinnerbaits. Pig 'n' jig or jig 'n' crawfish are good baits to cast for the deeper bass.

If you are willing to travel ten to twenty miles by boat, you can reach spots between Cleeses Ferry Ramps (one on each side of the river) and Nashville that are rarely fished. This is also true from Shelby Park ramp upstream.

Nashville angler David Woodward sums up how he fishes Cheatham: "Early morning, I start with a Tiny Torpedo or Devil Horse over points, six- to eight-foot shelves, drop-offs from twelve to twenty feet and eddies. As the sun gets higher, I switch to a do-nothing worm. I like the Swap Crawler. It looks like a nightcrawler and gets vicious hits. Later I go to two-tone worms or lizards. Near dark I use white and chartreuse buzzbaits with a white trailer, weedless rat, or frog."

Cheatham Lake is an untapped source for bass. The big question is, "Why don't more anglers fish here?"

Smallmouth Bass

Cheatham is a good fishery for smallmouth bass. They will spawn in gravel and mud areas in the backwater and along the creeks. After they spawn, look for them in the river and at creek mouths. Fish for them the way you would for largemouth bass (see above), especially with jigs.

Kentucky Bass

Kentuckies are present; they are up the creeks in the spring like smallmouth. When the creek water warms in June, they will move into the main river. Then you are as likely to catch a spotted as you are a largemouth or smallmouth.

Crappie

Cheatham offers a strong fishery for crappie. In the spring the creeks mentioned in the largemouth bass section will provide you with plenty of places to fish.

Crappie will take your small jigs and minnows as they do in other waters. Along the banks of these creeks, you will have ample opportunities to find downed trees and stumps. High water frequently resupplies the banks with crappie cover.

Summer fishing takes on another aspect. Crappie roam the deep channel banks of the Cumberland. Locating submerged trees on the channel is easy, and you are likely to find crappie among some of them. Since the water temperature is uniform in the main channel and warmer in the creeks, creek mouths may be as far as the fish will venture during the hot summer months.

Crappie hold on deep river channels in winter and may prove hard to find. Fish brush and submerged trees along the outside bend of the channel with a minnow-tipped jig. Move it slowly among the branches. If you don't get a hit within a few minutes, move on to another likely spot. The channel has so many places for crappie you need not spend much time in one area. When you find crappie, you will usually find many in one school.

Bream

As always, they are everywhere waiting for your worms or crickets. The prime areas are in the backwaters and creeks, at creek mouths, and in pockets along the banks and along the bluffs. A 2-pound, 8-ounce bluegill from Cheatham once held the state record. That lets you know there are some big bream in this lake.

Catfish

David Woodward recommends Sycamore, Bull Run, and Brush creeks for catfish. He says two- to eight-pound cats are commonly caught but twelve to fifteen pounders are not uncommon. Woodward says he catches between twenty and fifty cats from one to six pounds with minnows, chicken livers, and nightcrawlers near the tree line on Bull Run Creek and the creek mouth during the summer. Blue and channel cats are most often caught.

To catch the big flathead or yellow cats, Woodward fishes the deep ledges, rocky drop-offs, and eddies with large shiners or minnows. He recommends fishing near the twenty-foot depth.

Woodward warns anglers to drop anchor upstream from where they want to fish and let the bait drift downstream into the hole because, as he says, "Catfish are extremely spooky."

Walleye and Sauger

Sauger are more prevalent than walleye in Cheatham. From November to March you are likely to catch them at the mouths of the major tributaries. Minnows and jigs dressed with minnows fished on the bottom are the most effective methods. This is a good time to fish below all the dams in Middle Tennessee.

Once the spawn is over, around the end of March, sauger drift downstream and stay along the main river channel and where the river channel is joined by creeks. Fishing from sunset until dawn with top water imitation minnows, such as Rapala and Rebel, pays off in shallow water near the river channel. Cast downstream and "twitch" the minnow back to the boat. Shallows inside of the river's bend—the shallows just above or below a creek junction and humps, ridges, or bars in the river—are the likely night spots.

Trolling nightcrawler rigs with spinners or imitation minnow crankbaits is the most productive method for catching these fish during the summer. Troll the deep water on the outside river bends, ledges along the main channel, and deep water pockets at creek junctions.

TWRA added 56,000 inch-long sauger to the reservoir near Johnson Creek in 1991. "It's not the first time that the Cumberland system has received these particular fish, but it is the first time we have put them in Cheatham," says fisheries biologist John Riddle.

Rockfish and Hybrids

"Shiners and goldfish are legal bait on Cheatham," says David Woodward. "They are the best live bait to use for rockfish. The other best bait is a white quarter-ounce jig with a Sassy Shad. Drift these baits below schools of minnows you detect with your graph.

"I tie a 2/0 or 3/0 steel hook about eight inches above a one- to two-ounce sinker, depending on the current. With the minnow hooked through the lips, I put it just below the school of bait fish. I look at my graph to see that there are big fish below the school. If I don't see big fish, I don't fish that school. I move around until I find what I want.

"Sometimes those big fish under the baitfish are catfish or largemouth bass, I can't tell for sure until I catch one. But whatever it is, it's big enough to be fun."

Woodward says rockfish are usually found in twenty-five to thirty feet of water and occasionally nearer fifty feet. Below the dams are topnotch places to fish for stripers year round.

Some anglers cast cut shad from the bank into the swift water below the dam. They use several ounces of lead to keep the bait on bottom. Other anglers, using live or cut shad, run their boat into the swift water, then drift their bait on the bottom and downstream for a hundred yards. Both techniques are effective (*see* Tailwater section). Nine- to thirty-pound rockfish are common in Cheatham with some going forty pounds.

"We stock lakes on a per acre ratio, with each reservoir getting five fish per acre of water," says John Riddle. Cheatham received 56,500 striped bass in 1991. A total of 500,000 rockfish fingerlings were placed in Tennessee's reservoirs during the same year.

Stripe and Brassy Bass

These cousins, the white bass and the yellow bass, are often found together. The stripe grows larger than its brassy cousin but doesn't fight any harder. Yellow bass will weigh from one-half pound to a pound, and the white bass will weigh from one to two pounds in average catches.

Both hit the same baits—Little George, Rooster Tail, small jigs, and minnows. The fish are constantly moving and may be in five feet of water or twenty-five feet.

David Woodward recommends plying the mouths of Marrow-bone and Brush Creeks with small spoons or other lures resembling small shad. "Both of these fish are good table fare," he says.

BANK FISHING

Places with rip-rap and the submerged lock, like the Lock A Recreation Area, have good bank angling. The mouth of the Harpeth and the Harpeth River Recreation Area are accessible, as are Pardue Recreation Area and Sycamore Recreation Area. There are about three miles of bank to fish when you drive the route close to the river from Ashland City to Sycamore Creek. Northeast of Ashland City on TN 12, turn south at Marks Creek Bridge on Chapmansboro Road to follow the river by road.

Of course, where there are boat launches, there are places to bank fish—and usually good spots, too. Scout out several places on one side of the river one trip; then scout the other side the next time you go fishing.

FACILITIES

USACE and Other Agency Launching Ramps

Resource Manager: George Patterson, Route 5, Ashland City, TN 37015-9805 (615-792-5697 or 254-3734).

Cheatham Dam North Bank, from Ashland City north on TN 12, turn south at Cheap Hill onto Cheatham Dam Road; follow signs.

Lock A, camping available. *See* Cheatham Dam.

Sycamore Creek, north of Ashland City turn at Marks Creek Bridge off TN 12 onto old TN 12; follow signs.

Johnson Creek, south of Ashland City off TN 49 at Bellsburg; turn north; follow signs.

Pardue, south of Ashland City off TN 49, turn north past Harpeth River Bridge; follow signs.

Harpeth River Bridge, camping available. *See* Pardue.

Big Bluff Creek, south of Ashland City on TN 12; follow signs.

Bull Run Creek, south of Ashland City on TN 12 at Davidson–Cheatham County line; follow signs.

Brush Creek, near Ashland City on River Road (along Cumberland River between TN 49 south of Ashland City and Charlotte Pike in West Nashville).

Sam's Creek, east of Brush Creek on River Road. *See* Brush Creek.

Cleeses Ferry, north ramp—west of Nashville off TN 12 on Old Hickory Boulevard. South ramp—West Nashville off Charlotte Pike on Annex Road. Look for signs.

Shelby Park, East Nashville off Riverside Drive or Shelby Avenue from downtown; look for signs.

Commercial Campgrounds

Fiddlers Inn Campground, 2404 Music Valley Drive, Nashville, TN 37214 (615-885-1440). Off I-40, exit Briley Parkway (#215), north 4 miles to McGavock Pike exit, west to Music Valley Drive; look for signs. Near Priest, Old Hickory, and Cheatham lakes (via Old Hickory Dam).

Two Rivers Campgrounds, 2616 Music Valley Drive, Nashville, TN 37214 (615-883-8559). *See* Fiddlers Inn directions.

Yogi Bear's Jellystone Park, 1252 Highway 31W, Goodlettsville, TN 37072 (615-859-0348). Exit #98 off I-65, 1.5 miles north on US 31W; look for signs. Near Old Hickory and Cheatham lakes (via Old Hickory Dam).

Baitshops or Fishing Supplies

Crotty's Bait, 1577 Cheatham Dam Road, Ashland City, TN 37015 (615-792-7933).

Map Nine: Lake Barkley

CHAPTER SEVEN

LAKE BARKLEY

SEVENTY-FOUR OF BARKLEY'S 118 MILES ARE IN Tennessee. It is the last run-of-the-river lakes on the Cumberland River. It has 57,920 surface acres with 1,004 miles of shoreline at summer pool. Fall drawdown averages five feet, leaving a good amount of water for winter fishing: 45,210 acres. The river channel has a minimum depth of nine feet for navigational purposes. Depth near the dam is over sixty feet.

A canal, just over a mile long, connects Lake Barkley with Kentucky Lake near the dam offering convenience to boaters as well as commercial river traffic.

Barkley is very narrow from Cheatham Dam downstream for about fifty miles. Below Cumberland City, Tennessee, you will notice more backwater in the creeks. After the Cumberland crosses into Kentucky, about Saline Creek, it widens into a lake. The major tributaries offer good fishing in their backwaters.

When Kentucky anglers talk about the "lake," they are referring to the water from Barkley Dam south to the state line or slightly beyond. Dover, Tennessee, is at the southern end of the lake and serves as headquarters for Tennessee anglers, who fish this southern end to avoid buying a Kentucky license, and vice versa.

The major Kentucky tributaries from the dam upstream are Eddy Creek, Little River, Donaldson Creek, and Dry Creek. In Tennessee they are Saline Creek, North and South Cross creeks, Elk Creek, Guices Creek, Yellow Creek, and the Red River at Clarksville, which is the last major contributor to Lake Barkley.

From a line drawn west from Dover, Tennessee, to Kentucky Lake northward is the Land Between the Lakes (LBL) National Recreation Area. Its 170,000 acres have been set aside for outdoor activities from hiking, off-road vehicles, nature centers, and buffalo range to hunting, fishing, and camping.

Access to Barkley is easy from Clarksville, Tennessee, downstream to the dam. A total of fifty-five launching ramps spread out over its 118-mile run.

Fredda Lee, professional bass angler from Nashville, says, "If you don't know the lake, stay within the channel markers—you could run across a patch of stumps."

GAMEFISH SPECIES

Largemouth Bass

There are plenty of bass in this reservoir, even though crappie get most of the attention. Bass fishing is good all year long on Barkley. The northern end, from about Bumpus Mills or Saline Creek to the dam, has most of the best bass water. That's not to say there isn't good bassing in the rest of the river and creeks, but conditions are closer to ideal the last forty-five miles or so.

Tennessee anglers have an excellent section of the lake between Dover and Saline Creek. The productive creeks are Saline, Brandon Springs, Hickman, Lick, and Long. The hot spots downstream from Dover are North and South Cross creeks and Big Elk Creek.

Flippin' and pitchin' jigs or worms is an effective and popular method for luring bucketmouth into your boat. When bass are tight-lipped, a Carolina-rig can be persuasive. Fredda Lee says she prefers a three-fourth-ounce to one-ounce sinker. When you move the weight it makes an attracting noise and kicks up a little mud, the way a crawfish would when it scoots along the bottom.

Springtime on Barkley is crappie time. That means more traffic in the shallows. Bass anglers are in the minority during March and April but are undaunted because the best fishing is along the drop-offs.

Fredda says, "Bass move from deep water to mouths of creeks and bays first. Their second stage is from the primary points at the mouths to the secondary points. Their next stage is to spawn."

Cathy Summerlin is pleased to make the acquaintance of a largemouth bass caught in her secret fishin' hole.

Look for spring bass cover from five feet out from the bank to twenty feet along the edge of the drop-offs. These drops are along the river channel, creek channels, and coves. Use your graph to locate stump rows about five to fifteen feet deep along the larger channels.

"Bass move back into deep water in summer after they spawn," says Fredda, "along the channels and drop-offs." After bass recuperate from the spawn, which may last one to two weeks, they begin feeding with gusto. This is a prime time for catching lots of bass.

In summer, anglers fish creek mouths and the river channel. You can see schools of minnows orbiting the creek mouths, and the bass are nearby. There is usually current in the Cumberland, and the water is cooler than in the creeks—just what bass like. Another benefit of this cool water is that bass hang around the shallows all summer.

Buzz the logs, stumps, and floating cover with buzzbaits or topwater lures, such as the Tiny Torpedo or Devil Horse. Once you've tried the top, bump the cover with crankbaits. Shad Raps, Wee-Rs, or similar baits probe the mid-depths. Go with your worm to cover the bottom. If you believe bass should be there, start over and cast each bait fifteen to twenty times. If you haven't raised a bass by your fiftieth or sixtieth cast, that means it is suffering from "lockjaw," a condition normally associated with a frontal passage.

You can fish for hours and not take a bass, then limit out in minutes. Be patient and persistent.

Fredda says bass will repeat their spring movements in the fall. "They move back into the bays and creeks, stopping first at primary points, then secondary points. Then they move back into deep water for the winter."

Smallmouth Bass

The rocky northern end has a good fishery, and the places you fish for smallies won't vary much from places you catch largemouth. You may want to try jig 'n' pig or four-inch worms along the rocky or gravel areas. Gene Austin, a smallmouth specialist, says this fish will be where there is gravel and mud. Creeks usually have mud and gravel deposits at their mouths.

Smallmouth prefer cooler water than largemouth and will be around the main channel where there is some flow during the summer. Of course, the creek mouths such as Eddy Creek, Little River, Donaldson Creek, Dry Creek, and Saline Creek are good spots.

Kentucky Bass

It's better to refer to this bass as a Kentucky Bass rather than a spot or spotted bass that we are now fishing in that state. This bass has a strong population in Barkley.

Fish for them as you would for largemouth in smallmouth places. Look for stretches of rock or gravel, sloping points with rock or gravel, and big rocks. Fish the downstream side with jigs, crank-baits, and worms. After dark try topwater plugs in the creeks.

Crappie

King Crappie reigns on Barkley and nearby Kentucky Lake. A canal connects the two lakes, and the lower ends of the two lakes are very similar.

TWRA creel and netting reports show a strong crappie population, with about a 50-50 mix of black and white crappie. Most anglers catch white crappie because black crappie prefer clear and deeper water while anglers prefer fishing in shallow water.

White crappie like murky water and stay in the shallows longer. Barkley's best time for white crappie is in April and May.

The weather and water level determine which weeks are the best. Stable conditions, when the reservoir's water level isn't yo-yoing with heavy rains, are ideal for crappie fishing.

During the spring spawns, the black crappie come in earlier, around the third and fourth weeks of March, then depart for deeper water, says Ged Petit of TWRA. His observation over the last twenty years is that the white crappie will spawn later and remain in the shallows longer; in fact the medium-sized white crappie will stay year-round in about eight feet of water. Petit has watched his stakebeds over the years and has found this to be the case.

A majority of anglers use minnows under floats in the bushes and around the stumps and logs. More and more Barkley anglers are switching to jigs alone, one-thirty-second-ounce to one-sixteenth-ounce. These are fished from spinning reels, cane poles and crappie poles.

David Barber of Holladay, Tennessee, a part-time crappie guide on Kentucky Lake, says the eleven-foot B 'n' M crappie pole is his favorite, and it becomes his clients' favorite by the end of the day. Barber puts a small Medalist fly reel with six-pound golden Stren on his rods. He says to watch the line. Sometimes crappie barely move when they take the jig, and you have to be ready to set the hook when the line twitches.

Catching crappie in the spring is easy, but most anglers quit after that. Summer crappie are still ready to bite if you put your bait in the right place. The right place is along the drop-offs on the river and creek channels. Creek mouths are always good spots to try first during hot weather.

By fall, when the water cools, white crappie are likely to be in the shallows again, chasing threadfin shad and hanging around bushes, stumps, and logs, or whatever cover is available. Black crappie are still in the deeper water along the drop-offs waiting for your jigs and minnows.

Winter fishing is best along the main channels, tightlining minnows or jigs around crappie structure.

Some spots loaded with stumps that attract crappie are De-numbers, Davenport, Mammoth Furnace, Cravens, Fulton, and Honkers bays, and North Cross, McNabb, and Wells creeks, as well as the major creeks mentioned in the bass sections.

Catfish

Catfish are neglected at Barkley as in most of the other lakes. Channel, blue, and the bigger yellow cats live here, mostly undisturbed by the sports angler.

Rickey Groce landed a 65-pound, 8-ounce yellow cat in 1982 for the state record.

Springtime is best for catching cats in the shallows up the creeks and coves. Fish the sand and gravel bars with nightcrawlers, shad, minnows, chicken livers, and stinkbaits.

Use the same baits during the summer, when they are along the deep channels, except at night when they move on to shallow flats next to the channels.

Stripe

Wintertime below Cheatham Dam (*see* the Tailwater section) is bonanza time. The other cold-weather hot spots are the creeks. Stripe move around the mouth of creeks and upstream. Creek water is usually warmer than the main channel's water. However, some of the best stripe fishing—the bigger stripe—is just off the banks of the Cumberland.

Cast a white or chartreuse jig, one-eighth- to one-fourth-ounce, at a 45-degree angle upstream to the bank, then let it fall following the drop-offs to fill your boat. Stripe on Barkley like the steep clay-sandy banks on the outside of a bend. Anytime you can cast a jig so that it washes under a log jam be ready for a stripe strike.

Stripe are active in the headwaters of the Cumberland and larger tributaries in the spring until May. Then they move downstream or out into the main channel for the summer.

Summertime stripe angling is done by watching for the jumps. When the shad are being hit from below, you can cast small spoons, spinners, imitation minnows, and jigs into the fray and expect to catch several stripe before the action moves on. Trolling over sand and gravel bars and humps and around creek junctions with small, deep-diving crankbaits is effective.

When the water cools in the fall, stripe begin to move upstream. You can locate them with your graph, but they will be scattered.

Sauger and Walleye

Walleye are rare, so concentrate on sauger.

December through March is the easiest time to find and catch sauger. Beginning in November, they move upstream as part of their pre-spawn ritual. They lie on the bottom next to the main channel, creek, or river during daylight and move into the shallows to feed during the dark hours.

Jigs or jig 'n' minnow combos are the most reliable technique. Jigs, meaning two, are rarely used but are catching on. William Emerton of Sparta, Tennessee, puts two jigs to use and catches more fish than anyone in the headwaters of Center Hill Lake (*see* Center Hill's walleye section).

During the rest of the year, from June until November, troll the deep-water points, humps, and bars with a Tadpolly, Bagley's Walleye Shad, or a nightcrawler on a Hot 'n' Tot Pygmy to catch fish. Troll points at creek mouths that are steep on one side with a more gradual slope on the other and cast or jig the inside pockets of these points.

Bluegill

Springtime bedding is the best time to catch these fighters. From April through May they will be shallow along the flats near the channels and in the backs of sloughs and coves. Anglers who prefer fly rods can load their stringers using popping bugs in concert with the willowfly hatch.

Dropping crickets and red worms along the steep drop-offs and deep offpoints along the channel is effective during the summer months.

FACILITIES

Marinas

Green Turtle Bay Marina, Box 102, Ezzard Rock, Grand Rivers, KY 42045 (502-362-8364). Boat rentals, fishing supplies, ramp, food.

Leisure Cruise Marina, Box 191, Kuttawa, KY 42055 (502-388-7925). Cabins, boat rentals, fishing supplies, ramp, food.

Kuttawa Harbor, Kuttawa, KY 42055 (502-388-9563). Boat rentals, fishing supplies, ramp, food.

Eddy Creek Resort and Marina, Route 1, Eddyville, KY 42038 (502-388-7743). Cabins, boat rentals, fishing supplies, ramp, food.

Prizer Point Marina, Route 4, Cadiz, KY 42212 (502-522-3762). Cabins, camping, RV hookups, restaurant, more.

Lake Barkley Resort and Marina, Route 2, Cadiz, KY 42212 (502-

924-9954). Camping, RV hookups, restaurant, more.

Bumpus Mills Marina, Route 1, Box 46A, Bumpus Mills, TN 37028 (615-232-5238). Cabins, camping, RV hookups, restaurant, more.

USACE Launching Ramps (Camping Noted)

Resource Manager: Wayne Lanier, Lake Barkley, PO Box 218, Grand Rivers, KY 42045-0218 (502-362-4236).

Barkley Damsite, below dam.

Canal, camping. Off I-24 on The Trace (KY 453) near dam.

Eureka, camping. Northeast of dam on US 62.

Boyd's Landing, camping. North of Eureka.

Kuttawa, north of dam off US 62.

Eddyville, off I-24 on KY 93.

Eddy Creek, camping. Off KY 93 on KY 274.

Hurricane Creek, camping. South of Eddy Creek.

Cadiz, Off US 68 northeast of Cadiz.

Devils Elbow, camping. On east side of lake off US 68.

Linton, on Dry Creek off KY 164.

Bumpus Mills, camping. On Saline Creek off TN 120.

Blue Creek, north of Dover on east side of lake north off US 79.

Dyers Creek, across lake from Dover south off US 79.

Dover, west side of lake off US 79.

Hickman Creek, north of Dover off The Trace (TN 49), on west side of lake.

Other Access Areas (Including Parks)

Lake Barkley State Resort Park, southwest of Cadiz off US 68 on KY 1489.

Trice Landing, off US 79 south side of Clarksville, Tennessee.

McGregor Park, south of Trice Landing.

Buzzard Rock, off US 62 east of dam near Kuttawa.

Poplar Creek, east of Buzzard Rock.

Coleman Bridge, north of I-24 off KY 293.

Dryden Creek, off KY 274 between Eddy Creek and Little River.

Rivers End, north of mouth of Little River off KY 274.

Calhoun Hill, north side of Donaldson Creek off KY 164.

Donaldson Creek, south side of creek off KY 164.

Tobacco Port, north of Saline Creek off TN 120.

Saline Creek, off TN 120 near KY–TN border, northeast of Dover.

Lick Creek, off US 79 southeast of Dover.

Hematite, on TN 149, east of Cumberland City.

Mayberry Branch, off Hunley Road, southwest side of lake near Cheatham Dam.

Rivers Bend, off TN 149 north of Cumberland City.

Smith Branch, south off US 79 between Clarksville and Dover.

Nickell Branch, camping. South of Barkley Canal near dam, off The Trace (KY 453).

Denumbers Bay, south of canal off The Trace (KY 453). Continue south to locate (in order) *Kuttawa Landing, Eddyville Ferry, Cravens Bay* (camping), *Taylor Bay* (camping), *Devils Elbow, Bacon Creek, Neville Bay, Gatlin Point* (camping, three ramps).

Trigg County, on Hobson Creek off US 68 on east side.

Rock Castle, north of Trigg County off KY 274.

Little River, on KY 274 near bridge over Little River.

Guieses Creek, off TN 149 east of Cumberland City, Tennessee.

Commercial Campgrounds

Holiday Hills Resort, Route 1, Box 406, Eddyville, KY 42038 (502-388-7236). Cabins, RV hookups, dock, boat rental, store, more. South of Eddyville for 5 miles on KY 93. Exit 45 from I-24.

Indian Point, Route 2, Box 280, Eddyville, KY 42038 (502-388-2730). From I-24, take exit #45, go 1 mile. Dock, store, tents/RVs, more.

Tarryon Camping Resort, Route 1, Box 75-G, Kuttawa, KY 42055-9610 (502-388-7389). Full-service store, dock, more. West of exit #40 from I-24.

Spring Creek Campgrounds, 3050 Spring Creek Village Road, Clarksville, TN 37040 (615-645-2332). Exit #4 off I-24, one mile northeast on US 79; follow signs.

Baitshops or Fishing Supplies

The Headquarters Sportsman Center, Dover (615-232-6325).

B&J Bait Center, Dover Road, Clarksville (615-647-7874).

Busy Bee Bait Shop, Cumberland City (615-827-2755).

Ho-Jo's Mini Mart, Erin (615-289-4715).

J.T.'s Bait & Tackle, Indian Mound (615-232-6648).

Lakeland Bait & Tackle, Indian Mound (615-232-7431).

Jim's Market, Bumpus Mills (615-232-7149).

McCoy's Country Store, near Yorks Landing, Woodlawn (615-551-3663 or 645-9238).

Canton 1 Stop, Cadiz, Kentucky (502-924-5698).

Handy Korner Market, at Rockcastle on lake (502-522-3873).

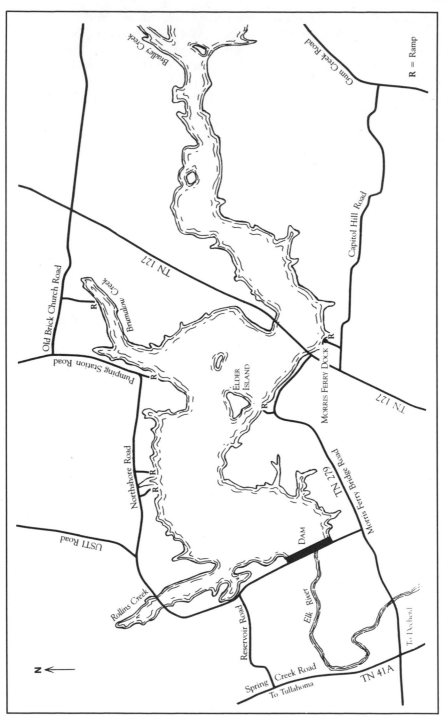

Map Ten: Woods Reservoir

CHAPTER EIGHT

WOODS RESERVOIR

WOODS RESERVOIR WAS COMPLETED IN 1952 by the U.S. Air Force to supply the Arnold Engineering Development Center (AEDC) with cooling water for its testing. It is a small lake on the Elk River that compares in size to Normandy Lake. Woods is twelve miles long with sixty-five miles of shoreline; it covers 3,980 acres.

Its major tributaries are the Elk River, Bradley Creek, Brumalow Creek, and Rollins Creek.

PCB pollution was discovered in the early eighties and a warning on catfish has been in effect since. The PCB levels are highest near the dam and are slowly dropping. Mrs. Della Norton of Morris Ferry Dock said she was told the level is presently about 2.5 parts per billion.

This level has been said to be as harmful as five cigarettes if you eat fifteen pounds of catfish a week from catfish weighing over fifteen pounds. This doesn't sound bad, but to be safe, limit your catfish intake to a pound or less a week of small catfish.

Woods is known as a "big" largemouth bass lake with plenty of crappie. Diverse structure is a plus for this lake, and there are TWRA-maintained fish attractors. The lower end of the lake, from Morris Ferry Bridge to the dam, is deep and wide with some steep points and drop-offs. Above the bridge is narrow and shallow with large flats and shallow coves and deep only in the Elk River channel.

Sid Price has been fishing Woods since 1975 and favors the upper end for bass and crappie, while guide Clyde Hill, Jr., favors the lower end for bass and crappie. Sounds like you can't go wrong.

There is one marina at Morris Ferry Dock, and there are five launching ramps.

GAMEFISH SPECIES

Largemouth Bass

Nine-pound bass are caught yearly, maintaining Woods' reputation for big largemouth bass. They are all over the lake, but the seasons play an important role.

The upper section of Woods warms fast under the springtime sun, and bass begin to take crankbaits in the shallows. Bradley Creek down to the bridge is the best early spring area. Cast around the brush and stumps in the coves on the north side of the lake. The bigger bass will come from coves and flats close to the Elk River channel, like the coves at mile 178 and mile 180. At mile 181 is Sid Price's favorite island for bass (*see* Appendix A for maps).

Bass action picks up in the lower section in early March. Brumalow Creek along the channel to Camp Arrowhead is a hot spot. Some anglers fish the area around Camp Arrowhead exclusively for lunkers.

Summer bassing becomes a nighttime sport after the water temperature climbs and the water clears. Casting jigs and worms along the channels and points, and working the coves close to the channel will yield bass in the four- to nine-pound range. Crankbaits, spinnerbaits, and worms take their share, not only in the these same areas but in the shallow areas away from the channel. The mouth of Brumalow Creek plays an important role in attracting and holding bass.

Bass break out again in the fall and feed heavily. The cool water spurs their appetite, and dingier water makes them feel safe enough to venture into the shallows again.

Wintertime angling produces bass off the points and rip-rap at the bridge by dangling a pig 'n' jig in front of the fish.

Smallmouth Bass

The best smallie action is in the lower end year-round. The rocky points and the bridge's rip-rap are hot spots. Probing the river

The author holding another of Woods Reservoir's strong fighters, a largemouth bass.

channel with one-eighth-ounce or one-fourth-ounce jigs with a green, orange, or black curlytail may result in your receiving a broken arm or having your rod snatched out of your hands. Small-mouth hit hard and fight hard, especially when you hang into a seven pounder.

Jigs are about the best smallie bait you can use, but try crawfish colored crankbaits and dark spinnerbaits around the rocky points, rip-rap, the pumping station at the mouth of Brumalow Creek, and the drop-offs between the dam and Camp Arrowhead.

Price says Hanover Bluff is about the best smallmouth spot on the lake and adds, "Woods is the best fishing lake in this part of the country."

Crappie

Woods is one of the best crappie lakes in Tennessee, and springtime is best—all over the lake. There are places anglers fish more than others, but crappie are everywhere. Rollins Creek is mentioned a lot, so are Brumalow Creek and the Camp Arrowhead area. The upper end is perhaps the best in early spring.

Above the Morris Ferry Bridge is the best structure for spawning crappie, large flats with stumps and brushy coves. Just dangle a jig or a minnow, and you are in the crappie business. The area above the bridge suffers from muddy water after heavy rains. White crappie like murky water, but if it becomes too muddy, try the big creeks in the lower end. Don't overlook the excellent opportunity that lies along the rip-rap at the bridge. This is sometimes the best spot on the lake.

Summertime crappie are deep along the Elk River channel. Price says to dunk a minnow at the fourth buoy near the channel out from Camp Arrowhead. When he says dunk, he means dunk it down to forty feet. The trees down there attract crappie.

Fall brings the fish to shallow water for a while. They are feeding on shad, so cast a small shad-colored bait along the shallow points and in the backs of creeks.

Wintertime crappie angling is like summertime angling—fish deep and in the same places.

Bream

As always, use worms and crickets in the coves during bedding season and in the deep spots along the bluffs during the summer. The warm months provide fly rodders good topwater action on popping bugs and foam-bodied spiders. In summer the dam's deep drop-offs are good spots for big bream.

Walleye

Woods is no longer the walleye lake it was in years past. Typical walleye trolling techniques along the river channel may be your best bet for hooking a toothy walleye.

Muskellunge

Muskie have not faired well in recent years. Della Norton said the biggest muskie in 1991 was 37.5 inches long and weighed twenty-one pounds. She keeps records of the top fish brought to her dock.

TWRA biologist Doug Pelren shocked up a keeper muskie while conducting a crappie study. The big fish came from a small cove in the upper end during April. Price says the best place to have a muskie attack your bait is from the pumping station to the mouth of Brumalow Creek.

TWRA put 500 toothy fingerlings in Woods in 1991. It takes about four years for these stocked fish to reach the legal limit length of thirty inches.

Woods Reservoir's muskie are tackle-busting fighters.

Catfish

A forty-two-pound blue cat was caught on rod and reel and brought to Morris Ferry Dock in the summer of 1991. It isn't uncommon to hang a really big cat in Woods during the summer.

The best cat holes are along the river channel for daytime fishing. Use your graph to locate ledges or deep drop-offs. Nightcrawlers, minnows, shad, liver, and stinkbaits are their preferred cuisine.

For night fishing, cast your offering into the shallow flats and coves near the dam, but stay close to the channel. Between the dam and Camp Arrowhead are several coves off the channel, and the flats off Camp Arrowhead point are good because this area is within a loop of the channel. The channel and the area around the bridge are also good spots for catfish.

BANK FISHING

The area around the lower end of Woods is well developed, and many sites are available for anglers on foot. You can reach most of the lower end of the lake by roads; improved and unimproved roads will give you access to the upper end. Most of the shoreline is walkable. Fishing at the dam is easy, above and below.

FACILITIES

Marina and Ramps

Morris Ferry Dock, Route 2, Box 144, Estill Springs, TN 37330 (615-967-5370). Dock, gas, fishing supplies, camping, nightly to monthly rentals, ramp. Store closed November 20–March 1 but rentals available. From I-24 take exit #117, go 6 miles, off TN 127 south of Morris Ferry Bridge on Capitol Hill Road, on left.

Franklin County Park, ramp. East from TN 127 on Morris Ferry Bridge Road; turn at sign.

Brumalow Creek, ramp. AEDC exit from I-24; follow signs to Old Brick Church Pike, turn south to Coffee County Recreation Area.

Pumping Station Ramp, ramp. Go south off AEDC Road on Pumping Station Road.

Two Ramps, west of pumping station on Northshore Road about 1 mile, look for roads leading south to ramps. From the dam, ramps are about 1 mile east from Rollins Creek Bridge on Northshore Road.

Campgrounds

Foster Falls Small Wildlife Area, call TVA Recreation Program (615-632-1600). Exit #134 off I-24 at Monteagle, TN, 56 to Tracy City, south on TN 150 for 5 miles; follow signs.

Jim Oliver's Smokehouse Campground, PO Box 579, Monteagle, TN 37356 (615-924-2268). Exit #134 off I-24, west on US 64 for 300 yards. From Woods, Manchester is 10 miles north; Tullahoma, 6 miles east; Winchester, 5 miles south. *See* Normandy Lake and Tims Ford Lake chapters.

Baitshops or Fishing Supplies

The Sportsman, Tullahoma (615-455-0354).

Tackle Shack, Tullahoma (615-393-4320).

CHAPTER NINE

NORMANDY LAKE

SITUATED ON THE UPPER DUCK RIVER, NOR-
mandy is a 3,230-acre TVA lake with seventy-two miles of shoreline
and a seventeen-mile length built for flood control. It is a highland
lake with six launching ramps. It has no marinas, but camping is
available.

The wide lower end, from the dam to the bridge, is the deepest
part of the lake. It is ninety feet deep in front of the dam. From the
bridge upstream, the lake narrows. The major tributaries are the
Duck River and Riley, Carroll, and Crumpton creeks.

The banks are steep, with a few sloping points; but most of
Normandy's banks drop off fast. Areas of standing timber along the
channel and in the creeks provide good cover for bass and crappie.

GAMEFISH SPECIES

Largemouth Bass
Normandy is known as a largemouth bass lake. Casting crankbaits and jigs along the rip-rap at the dam and bridges is very
productive in the spring, as are the backs of the creeks. In addition
to fishing the usual bass techniques and structures, work the shallow
areas along undercut banks with spinnerbaits and crankbaits first,
then with jigs and worms.

Normandy's deep creek channels make this a good reservoir for
springtime trolling. The Hot 'n' Tot Pygmy with a nighcrawler will

99

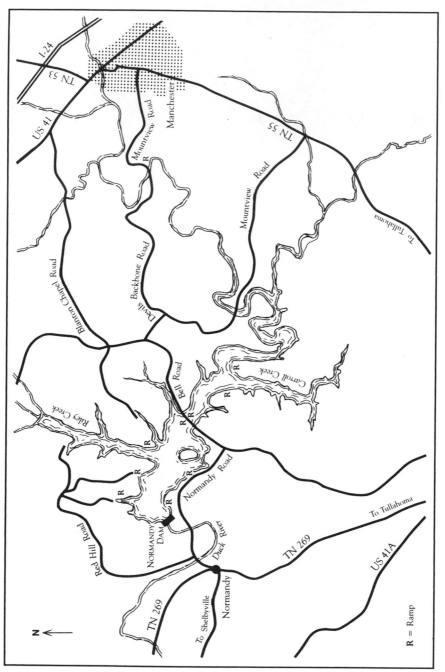

Map Eleven: Normandy Lake

R = Ramp

N

I-24
TN 53
US 41
Mountview Road
Manchester
TN 55
Mountview Road
To Tullahoma
Blanton Chapel Road
Backbone Road
Devils
Carroll Creek
Bell Road
Riley Creek
R
R
R
R
R
R
R
R
Normandy Road
Red Hill Road
NORMANDY DAM
Duck River
To Shelbyville
Normandy
TN 269
TN 269
To Tullahoma
US 41A

catch other fish species as well as bass. Other lures good for trolling are deep-diving crankbaits and spoons.

Summer bass are taken deep along the main channel and creek channels on summer days. Worms, jigs, and jigging spoons work well along these steep channel drop-offs. Spinnerbaits and topwater plugs work well in the shallows at night. Fish the points and flats around the points and islands first; then move up the creeks to fish the cuts in the banks and both sides of the bends in the creeks. There isn't much current in the big creeks, but try the smaller feeder creeks after a rain for improved summertime action.

In the fall look for bass in the shallows and near the creek mouths with schools of shad. By October they are hitting strong during the daylight hours. During the fall drawdown, more current is generated in the creeks, and it is a good time to fish the banks along the big creek mouths. Watch for bass in the jumps. The draw-down is about sixteen feet.

Wintertime bass are deep, and trolling the channels is effective. The most effective way to take the cold, lethargic bass is by jigging. Work a jig 'n' pig or Carolina-rigged worm among the trees and stumps in the deepest part of creek mouths at their junctions with the Duck River.

With the TVA map of Normandy (*see* Appendix A) you can locate ruins, culverts, submerged bridges, rocks, stumps, standing timber, and many other structures where bass hold.

Smallmouth Bass

The rocky Duck River channel above Barton Springs is an excellent place to stalk the smallie. They prefer moving water with a rocky or gravel bottom. They aren't strictly limited to this area and are found throughout the lake, thanks to its deep cool water.

Fish the rocky points, banks, and channel with one-eighth-ounce jig 'n' pig and small crankbaits. The rocky area at the mouth of Boyd Branch, the rip-rap at the head of Riley Creek and at the bridge, the rocky area below the Ward Chapel Road ramp, and the rip-rap at the Ward Chapel Road bridge (Anthony Bridge) are good smallie spots.

February to May and October to November are prime smallie months. Fish for the bronzebacks as you would in Dale Hollow or Center Hill during the spring and fall, deep with jigs.

Smallmouth tear up the topwater feeding on baitfish in the fall. Make long casts beyond the surface activity to avoid spooking the feeding fish. Bring your bait through the jumps; as your lure reaches the activity, let it stop and fall like an injured shad; then be ready for a smashing hit.

Kentucky Bass

There is a strong Kentucky bass population in Normandy. Look for them in all the places you would look for largemouth and smallmouth bass. They like small crawfish-colored crankbaits.

Crappie

Normandy has an excellent fishery of black and white crappie. Fish the standing timber and stumps in the major tributaries in all but the spawning months, which are from March to May. Look for shallow water in the creeks during their spawn. Riley and Carroll creeks have good crappie spots. Springtime frontal passages drive crappie back into the timber, so fish there if you don't find them in the shallows.

Black crappie like deeper, clearer water and prefer rocks and vegetation, whereas white crappie prefer shallow, murky water around logs and stumps.

Carroll Creek has a lot of stumps at its mouth along the river channel and the creek channel. Two hot spots in Carroll Creek are where Copperas Branch and Bobo Creek join it. Use your graph to locate the timber and stumps.

Saugeye

Tennessee Wildlife Resources Agency stocked the lake with walleye in the eighties, but they didn't take. They later began a saugeye stocking program that has taken off. Anglers can expect to catch five- to eight-pound saugeye now.

TWRA fisheries biologist Doug Pelren said they stack up in front of the dam during the winter, and floods wash them over the dam, stocking the Duck for miles downstream. He said the saugeye are "put and take" since they are sterile hybrids, a cross between the walleye and sauger.

Trolling points, depressions, humps, and channels with deep-diving crankbaits or nightcrawlers in front of the dam during the cold-water months and working the bottom with jigs are good techniques.

Trolling the steep banks along the channels of Riley Creek and the Duck River is a good warm weather technique.

Bream

Beginning in April, when bream go on the bed until September, you can load your boat with bluegill, warmouth, and sunfish. Use crickets and worms for fishing the beds and deep water, and use popping bugs for topwater action. Fish in the gravel and sandy areas of creeks for bedding bream and along the rocky banks during the summer.

Stripe

Normandy Lake is a growing stripe fishery but is not prominent at this time. Fish the headwaters in February and March using small spoons, spinners, and jigs. In the summer look for jumps. Other times of the year, troll the points with small diving lures.

Catfish

An earlier stocking of blue catfish didn't take, but TWRA dumped 30,000 more into the lake in 1991. There are some yellow and channel cats but not a strong fishery.

BANK FISHING

Bank fishing is easy at the six ramps, on the rip-rap at the bridges, and along the rip-rap at the dam. There are many roads that dead-end in the lake. Locate these roads with a TVA map (*see* Appendix A) or county maps. Fishing is limited at some of these sites because high banks prevent easy access to the water; however, fishing the edge of roadbeds is a good way to catch bass and bream.

FACILITIES

TVA Facilities and Ramps

Barton Springs, TVA Recreation Program (615-632-1600). Ramp, camping, swim beach, picnic areas (shelters/grills). East of dam on Normandy Road.

Cedar Point, TVA Recreation Program (615-632-1600). Ramp, camping, swim beach, picnic areas (shelters/grills). North off Normandy Road, west of dam on Red Hill Road, turn east at first junction; follow signs.

Damsite, ramp off Normandy Road between Barton Springs and the Duck River Bridge below dam.

Boyd Branch, ramp. Follow directions to Cedar Point; Boyd Branch Road turns south to lake before Cedar Point Road.

Ward Chapel Road, ramp. Take Powers Bridge Road east from Manchester, turn on Ward Chapel Road. (Devils Backbone Road on some maps); follow signs.

Powers Bridge, ramp. Take Powers Bridge Road east from Manchester; follow signs.

Commercial Campgrounds

Manchester KOA, PO Box 870, Manchester, TN 37355 (615-728-9777). Exit #114 off I-24, turn west.

Old Stone Fort State Park, Route 7, Box 7400, Manchester, TN 37355 (615-728-0751). Exit #110 off I-24, west to US 41, then one-half mile north; entrance on left.

Whispering Oaks, Route 2, Box 2760, Manchester, TN 37355 (615-728-0225). Exit #105 off I-24, south 0.4 mile, then west 0.7 mile on paved road.

To get to Normandy Lake from Manchester, go south on TN 55, turn west on Ward Chapel Road (also called Wilson Boulevard). From Tullahoma, go north on US 41 Alt, turn east on TN 269 to Normandy community; follow Normandy Road to lake. From Shelbyville, go west on US 41 Alt; turn east on Normandy Road to lake.

Baitshops or Fishing Supplies

Dragonfly Bait Shop, south of Shelbyville on US Alt 41 (615-684-2839).

Tackle Shack, Tullahoma (615-393-4320).

Custom Tackle Supply, south of Shelbyville on US Alt 41 (615-684-6164).

The Sportsman, Tullahoma (615-355-0354).

J&D Market, Manchester (615-728-1275).

CHAPTER TEN

TIMS FORD LAKE

TIMS FORD IS A TVA LAKE. IT IS IN THE BARrens of Tennessee just below the Cumberland Plateau in Franklin and Moore counties. A short distance downstream from Woods Reservoir on the Elk River, Tims covers 10,700 acres, has 241 miles of shoreline, and is 34 miles long. It is over 150 feet deep and has a fall draw-down of 23 feet.

The major tributaries include the Elk River and Rock, Boiling Fork, Hurricane, Little Hurricane, and Lost creeks. Lost and Hurricane creeks are long, little lakes in themselves. There are markers at the mouths of most of the creeks identifying them by name.

The communities of Decherd and Winchester are on Boiling Fork Creek. Use caution when power boating up this creek because of shallow areas. About two miles below Woods Reservoir Dam is the town of Estill Springs with similar shallow water hazards.

Striper guide Jim McClain says Tims Ford's water is in good shape. McClain is also a wildlife officer for the Tennessee Wildlife Resources Agency. If you are interested in learning to catch rockfish, get his video "Striper Secrets on Tims Ford." Look for it in *Trophy Striper* magazine and places that sell outdoor videos.

There are ten public launching ramps, including one state park and two marinas; however, there are many unimproved lake access points. The access points are distributed throughout the lake, making boat launching convenient to all areas.

Tims is similar to other highland lakes like Dale Hollow and Center Hill in possessing many deep, long creeks, numerous coves

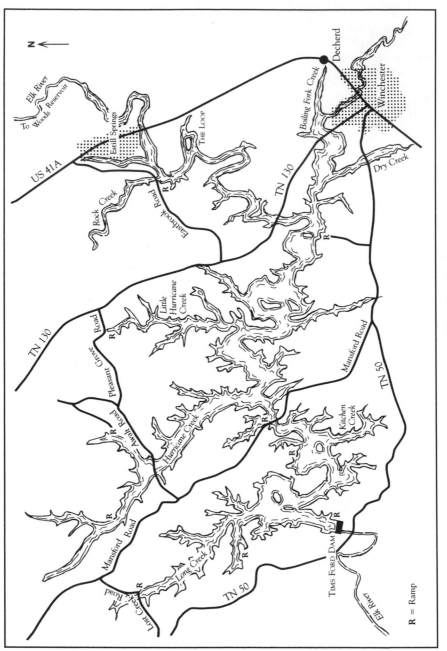

Map Twelve: Tims Ford Lake

R = Ramp

and bays, steep drop-offs, rocky clay banks, and great fishing.

Fish attractors are employed on Tims. They have been shown to hold nineteen times more crappie than open water and nine times more largemouth bass than you would find in open water. Look for white buoys with the orange fish symbol. One buoy locates the center of a half-acre brush pile, while two buoys will mark the two ends of a long brush pile.

You can find these attractors in Turkey, Hurricane, Anderton, Anderson, Boiling Fork, Rock, Dry, and Kitchens creeks, in Hatchet and Travis hollows, and along the Elk River channel near Cline Ridge, Marble Plains Church, Jollys Rock, Leatherwood Island, West Maple Bend, the junction of Boiling Fork Creek, Blackwood Hollow near Copperas Cave, and Estill Springs Park (*see* Appendix A for map of fish attractors and Appendix C for guides).

GAMEFISH SPECIES

Largemouth Bass

Bigjaws like rock and wood. These two items are abundant in the creeks and coves, and creeks and coves are bountiful on Tims. So, where to start? Keep in mind that bass like a deep-water access that could be the main channel or a creek channel. Find a cove with this deep-water avenue, and you have a place to start. Bass guide Gene Austin suggests Dry Creek.

You can locate deep water on the outside of a channel's bend, at creek junctions, and under bluffs. For instance, the bluffs on the east side of the mouth of Hurricane Creek have coves at each end and are good spots to try. Don't be surprised if you catch a smallie while angling for bigmouth in these places.

The backs of rock and wood coves are hot springtime spots. As the water warms, you can move down the creeks and keep busy from March until June cranking in bass.

Once the water warms and clears, switch to night fishing. The black lights attached to your boat gunwale allow you to watch your line in the dark. Stren's fluorescent lines prove their worth under the black lights because you can see them very well. Dark-colored jigs and worms are the best baits for fishing the steep banks at night.

Fall fishing is excellent. Bass feed on shad in the jumps. When there is some color up the creeks, bass take spinnerbaits in the shallows. Look for a mudline and cast so that your bait swims along the seam. Bass hide in the colored water and swim out to take baitfish coming close.

Use a light line, six-pound test, for casting crankbaits in the clear fall water. Cast deep divers such as the Deep Wee-R, Countdown Rapala, Shad Rap, or Hellbender to cover the points. Cast to the inside pocket of the points, as well as across them.

During the cold-water months, work slow-moving baits like jigs and worms along the channels. Fish various depths until you find their pattern, which could be twelve feet deep or forty feet deep. Bass do not respond to bait worked very fast in cold water, so your presentation has to accommodate them—slow is the key.

Smallmouth Bass

Oooooo-weeee! That describes Tims' smallie action. Mr. Number One Sportfish thrives within Tims' rocky shores. All the bronzeback you could ask for is here: crayfish among the rocks, clean, cool water with a long growing season, and plenty of forage fish.

Springtime is like heaven to brown bass enthusiasts. Casting a one-eighth-ounce jig dressed in a Power Craw can't be beat for taking smallies from the rocky points. Guide Gene Austin says to look for red clay and gravel banks for the hot smallie spots. He says he would start at Kitchens Creek or Little Hurricane Creek.

Late February marks the beginning of smallie season. They begin to stir in the shallows before largemouth. By mid-March take precautions not to let those seven-pounders break your arm. They will be hitting crawfish crankbaits like Bass Magnets by Bass Hunter Lures, Rebel's Deep Wee Crawfish, and Bill Norman's Quarterback or Jointed Doo-Dad. A smallmouth killer lure you don't see used much is Mepp's Minnow—it can entice a smallie when nothing else will.

If you stay with the four-inch Power Craw on a one-eighth- or one-fourth-ounce jig or rigged Texas style, you have the best smallie bait for year-round use day or night. The one exception is when smallies are in the jumps. Johnson's Silver Minnow, Floating Rapala, Tiny Torpedo, or Pop-R should hang you a jumping bass.

Remember—clear water, thin line. Tims turns clear in the summer, and if you fish during the day, you need to downsize your line. Night fishing doesn't require thinner line, just fluorescent.

Fall fishing brings the bass back to the shallows, and crankbaits and spinnerbaits will work again. But keep jigging the points, especially the ones at the ends of bluffs and where there are gravel and clay.

Since smallmouth are willing wintertime fighters, fish deeper during the cold-water months.

Kentucky Bass

Not sought after like its larger cousins, the spot is present in Tims. As in all of Middle Tennessee's lakes, you will catch them with the same baits and in the same places as you catch the other black bass.

Rockfish

This fish is becoming Tims' most popular gamefish. Like the smallmouth, it has excellent growing conditions—cool, clean water and plenty of forage. At this writing, there are rockfish weighing fifty pounds; the lake record is 49 pounds, 8 ounces.

Let's start fishing for linesides in the upper end and up the major creeks. When the water cools to about 60 degrees, rockfish get the urge to spawn, and as is their nature, they move to the headwaters to carry out their hormones' demands. Hessey Branch, Rock Creek, and Taylor Creek mouths and the Elk River at the Estill Springs Bridge are the hot spots during the cold weather.

Trolling shad is usually the most productive method. Slowly troll up the river channel from The Loop near Hessey Branch up to the bridge, and give each creek mouth thorough coverage. Closer to the dam, the headwaters of Hurricane Creek and the mouths of Lick and Turkey Creeks hold stripers.

Other techniques include casting shad-colored plugs, deep-diving to topwater. Diving plugs or crankbaits are cast to the points close to the channel; the same points should receive a thorough casting of topwater baits.

Try trolling spoons, such as Hopkins' Smoothie, Johnson's large Silver Minnow, a Red Eye Spoon, and Acme's Kastmaster Bucktail, instead of shad or bluegill. When you have a school located, you can try jigging those spoons among the fish. The same is true for jigs. Jigging, casting, or trolling heavy jigs (one-half to one ounce) with steel hooks dressed in a white grub or curlytail works very well when you see the big fish on your LCG.

By April stripers are busting topwater lures and continue to make raids in the shallow strata for forage until late May. Redfin has been the most popular topwater lure over the years, but there is no reason Rapala, Rebel, Storm, Bagley, and other big minnow imitators wouldn't do as well.

Come summer, downriggers are the thing. Tims Ford striper guide Jim McClain uses four downriggers to which he can run six rods. With the assistance of eight-pound cannonballs, he can place his bait—shad, jigs, or plugs—in the strike zone of the rockfish he sees on his graph.

He employs three live-bait techniques:

1. Down rod—a 3/0 steel hook for bluegill or shad and a three-eighth-ounce weight three feet above the hook. This is dropped down just above the rockfish so the swimming bait is in the correct position for a strike.
2. Free line—the bait is hooked and thrown out to swim freely among the rockfish.
3. Balloon fishing—a balloon bobber is tied to the line with a slip knot. The balloon is used with the other two methods, down rod and free line.

Jim uses fifteen-pound test Big Game Trilene line, and his biggest fish weighed thirty-eight pounds.

Summer and fall are trolling time on Tims, but after the water cools, the big stripers resume their surface raids on the now large schools of shad. Tie on a Redfin, a ThunderStick, or another choice of big topwater plugs, and make long casts to the jumps. If you get too close, the stripers will sound, and you will have to wait for them to reappear, usually too far away to make a cast.

As winter moves in the fish move too. Look to the headwaters, and begin the cycle anew.

Crappie

Both black and white crappie are found in Tims. Crappie action picks up in February and peaks in the shallows in April.

During the white crappie spawn, fish in the backs of coves where there is shallow structure near a soft bottom. Black crappie spawn sooner than the whites, and they spawn deeper over gravel in a soft bottom.

The three most productive methods for springtime angling are jigs, jig with a minnow, or a plain minnow on a 1- to 2/0-wire hook under a float. Fish from two feet to eight feet deep from the end of March until the middle of May. For those of you who like to see structure, try the upper end, where plenty of structure is visible.

Use a graph at the lower end to locate crappie cover along the banks and in the coves.

When the water is summer-warm or winter-cold, tightline jigs or minnows off points, drop-offs, channels, and submerged trees on the deep flats. The creeks near the dam are the best areas in the summer, whereas deep creeks up lake are good wintertime spots. Don't forget all those fish attractors—they hold crappie.

Fishing under the lights is the best summertime method. A submerged light or a strong beam pointed down will attract baitfish, which in turn attract crappie and other predatory species. Tightlining minnows and pumping jigs or spoons among the forage are productive techniques.

Bream

As with crappie, spring bream fishing begins in the backs of coves and creeks in shallow areas. Bream go on the bed later than crappie but may overlap some. Springtime baits are worms, small minnows, and small jigs. Since bream hit when there is little movement in the bait, retrieve jigs slowly.

Summer fishing is best along the rocky banks near deep water. Crickets and worms are the ticket. Fly fishing is good with foam-bodied spiders, terrestrial imitations, nymphs, and popping bugs early and late in the day.

Catfish

The waters below Woods Reservoir Dam down to Boiling Fork Creek are prime for spawning catfish. Channel, blue, and yellow cats spawn from May into July. The heads of creeks off the main lake are the other good spots during these months.

During July, August, and part of September you will have to fish the deep creek channels during the day and locate shallow flats off the deep water for night fishing. Stinkbaits, liver, shad (alive or cutbait), nightcrawlers, and big shiners are proven choices.

BANK FISHING

The upper end is more hospitable to the bank angler, especially the parks (see below), commercial areas, and ramp areas. Most of Tims' banks are steep and difficult to reach on foot.

FACILITIES

Marinas and Launching Ramps

Holiday Marina, PO Box 1556, Tullahoma, TN 37388 (615-455-3151). Cabins, camping, motel, restaurant, fishing supplies, boat rental, ramp. South of Tullahoma off Await Center Grove Road on Lick Creek.

Tims Ford Marina and Resort, Route 4, Box 4302, Winchester, TN 37398 (615-967-4509). Cabins, boat rentals, restaurant, groceries, guide service, ramp. East of Winchester off TN 50, turn north on Mansford Bridge Road; past the bridge, turn right.

Tims Ford State Rustic Park, Route 4, Winchester, TN 37398 (615-967-4457). Marina—operated by Betty and Johnny Riddle (615-967-9668 or 455-9987)—with restaurant, supplies, boat rental, groceries, guide service, ramp. Park offers more than a good place to fish. East of Winchester off TN 50, turn north on Mansford Bridge Road, left past the bridge at the sign.

Lost Creek Ramp, southwest from Tullahoma on TN 55 through Lynchburg, east on TN 50, turn left on Possum Trot Road, turn left on Lost Creek Road, cross bridge and turn right.

Anderton Creek Ramp, directions to Lost Creek, but stay on Possum Trot Road until you see sign for Anderton ramp.

Turkey Creek Ramp, south from Tullahoma on Gourdneck Road; follow signs.

Rock Creek Ramp, east of Estill Springs on Eastbrook Road, just across bridge.

Devils Step Ramp, east of Winchester, north off TN 50 before crossing bridge below dam.

Pleasant Grove Ramp, south of Tullahoma, east of Winchester Road, south of Pleasant Grove Road.

Baitshops or Fishing Supplies

Broadview Grocery, Route 4, Winchester (615-967-3097).

Dry Creek Bait & Tackle, on TN 50 near Devils Step Ramp, Winchester (615-962-0902).

Lost Creek Bait Shop, Lost Creek Road, Lynchburg (615-759-4199).

All Ashore Store, Eastbrook Road, Estill Springs (615-649-2383).

Tackle Shack, Tullahoma (615-393-4320).

PART TWO

TAILWATER FISHING

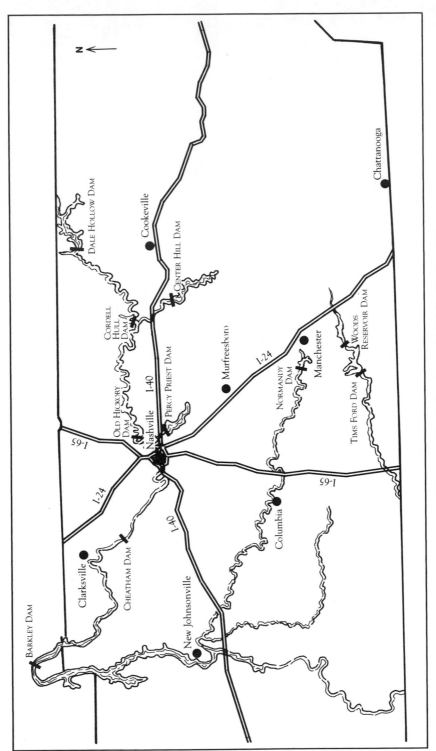

Map Thirteen: The Tailwaters of Middle Tennessee

THE TAILWATERS

TAILWATERS OR TAILRACES ARE THE AREAS below dams where the water races downstream after being freed from the upstream reservoir. Water is released via spillways during floods but more frequently from the turbines generating hydro-electric power.

The water is funneled from the lake to the top of a turbine where its tremendous pressure spins the turbine blades. This is where anglers become interested in the process. The spinning blades provide us with chum.

Baitfish are sucked in with the lake water, chopped up, or at least stunned, and discharged with the racing water. Fish have learned a free lunch is waiting for them during these periods of generation. The following chapters tell how to capitalize on this phenomenon.

Many anglers are apprehensive about fishing below dams and are aware of at least one horror story about a boat being "sucked under." Fishing in front of the turbine discharge area is dangerous. The signs say so.

The sudden upward rush of water through the turbine vent can cause a vortex of great force that pulls down momentarily. Once the flow is established, boats are tossed about on top of the boils. When I experienced this, I was lucky enough to escape without physical harm; however, my mental state required weeks to recover. To this day I maintain a healthy fear of the water's awesome power.

Call for the generation schedule of the dam you intend to fish. The numbers are listed at the end of Appendix A. These schedules are subject to change without warning. Be alert and careful. Most dams do not have warning devices but soon may if the Corps of Engineers' safety project at Center Hill Dam is successful.

Care and good sense are your two main safety assets. Another is a life vest, which the law now requires you to wear if you are in a boat below a dam. It is an excellent idea to wear one even if you are only wading or bank fishing below a dam.

When the water is released, it comes in a powerful wave that can take you by surprise. You will get along fine if you keep your attention focused on the water and on what you are doing.

Fishing below dams is my favorite. Dams are the end of the stream, the headwaters as far as a fish is concerned. Usually there are pools where fish congregate and feed. Tailraces attract many species of fish, some only during periods of hydroelectric generation, some during the spring, and others that live there year-round. A tailrace offers diverse opportunities to the angler.

I have selected eight tailwaters to fish because of their unique qualities and for the species of fish each has to offer. I will describe fishing techniques that are effective and point out some spots where I have caught fish or that I have learned about from reliable sources. I hope these honey holes are good to you.

CHAPTER ELEVEN

DALE HOLLOW DAM

DALE HOLLOW DAM WAS THE FIRST OF THE ten dams designed by the U.S. Army Corps of Engineers and built in the Nashville District. This flood control project on the Obey River was completed in 1943, and its hydroelectric capabilities were added later.

Seven miles downstream, the Obey River joins the Cumberland River in the upper reaches of Cordell Hull Lake.

From the tailrace you will see the three generators on the left side of the dam between two guard walls. To the right of that are the spillways. The bottom of the Obey is solid rock covered with algae. During periods of low water, the depth will vary from a few inches in front of the spillway to about eight feet in front of the generators. During generation the water rises between three and ten feet, depending on the number of generators used.

Most angling is done from the bank, but canoes and john boats are appropriate for low-water conditions. Motorboats can operate below the dam during high water. These boats should leave soon after generation ceases, or they will become stranded until the next generation period. The launching ramp is on the north bank off TN 53. Look for signs pointing toward the dam, campgrounds, hatchery, and ramp.

The north bank is readily accessible to the bank angler from the parking lot and campgrounds. It becomes steeper downstream from the launching ramp but still walkable.

The south bank can be reached by wading across the shallow

Obey River. Many anglers stand in the middle of the stream in waders. The bottom is slippery, and a wading staff is helpful. Some of the south bank is steep, but near the dam it flattens for easy walking.

The wonderful thing about the tailwaters is the trout fishing it offers. The U.S. Fish and Wildlife service operates a trout hatchery on the banks of the lower Obey River. Brown and rainbow trout are grown in long, narrow concrete tanks at the rate of 210,000 pounds a year. There are twenty rainbows for every brown trout.

Founded in 1977, this facility is the southernmost trout hatchery in the U.S. The eggs come from brood trout living in the northeast and are hatched here. The trout are fed something like "trout chow" until they are large enough to be released.

The facility is being enlarged to produce 300,000 pounds of trout annually. This enlargement, unfortunately, is not expected to meet the demand for trout by the year 1994.

The reason the U.S. Fish and Wildlife began operation here was to replace the native fish species displaced by the damming of streams. The displaced fish were replaced with species that would survive in the colder water that comes from the bottom of the lake.

The temperature of the water from the dam runs about 47 degrees. This cold water has an effect on downstream lakes along the Cumberland River. The effects, however, are greatly diminished by the time the water reaches Old Hickory Dam.

Dale Hollow's tailwaters contain rainbow and brown trout and rockfish on a put-and-take basis. Native species are largemouth and smallmouth bass, stripe, sauger, and walleye. A few lake trout are caught, but they came from stocking above the dam.

In 1969 the state's record for cutthroat trout was caught below the dam—it weighed six ounces. In 1971 a record trout of larger proportions was caught. This was a 14-pound, 8-ounce rainbow caught by Jack Rigney.

Below Dale Hollow and Center Hill dams are the most popular trout fisheries in Middle Tennessee. Dale Hollow is not as deep, nor does it have a constant flow of water as has Center Hill (see Center Hill Dam chapter). But Dale has a constant supply of trout.

Most anglers catch these stocked trout with nightcrawlers and corn. Fly anglers do well also, and they are not bothered by thick algae covering their bait. The algae doesn't seem to bother the trout because hundreds are caught a month.

A view of Dale Hollow Dam from the Obey River, the site of two state trout records.

When the water rises, more fish species and larger fish come upstream to the dam. The trade off is that to catch bigger fish you must learn to fish in the swift, high water. Fishing is much easier during non-generation periods, but the fish are more aloof.

FACILITIES

Camping
Dale Hollow Dam. Contact Resource Manager Franklin Massa, Route 1, Box 64, Celina, TN 38551-9708 (615-243-3136). Bath houses, RV dumping station, picnicking, ramp.
For other nearby accommodations see Dale Hollow Lake chapter.

CHAPTER TWELVE

CORDELL HULL DAM

THERE ARE THREE LAUNCHING RAMPS BELOW Cordell Hull Dam. One is accessed in Carthage below the TN 25 bridge and is a five-mile trek upstream to the dam but is close to the mouth of the Caney Fork River. The other two ramps are on opposite banks below the dam. The west bank ramp is accessed by going through Carthage on TN 263 and following the signs. The east bank ramp is accessed by going east from Carthage on US 70N and turning north on Horseshoe Bend Road and following the signs.

The mouth of the Caney Fork River, between Carthage and the dam, is a productive fishing area. The same species of fish are caught at the mouth of the Caney Fork as below the dam.

The dam is 769 feet wide. The powerhouse section houses three generators, and this is a dangerous area during periods of generation. The spillway section is 291 feet wide with five spillways. The last section is the lock, 168 feet wide.

The water level varies with seasons and generation schedules. With that in mind, here are a few relative depths. In front of the powerhouses you will find depths of thirty feet. At the junction of the powerhouse wall and the spillway, there is an abrupt rise to seventeen-foot depth that continues to the lock wall. There is a two-foot step-up from that seventeen-foot depth that runs from the lock to the powerhouse.

The lock wall bulges out irregularly toward the discharge area. It is twenty feet deep next to that wall and rises to fourteen feet deep toward the main channel, then falls back to twenty feet deep. Fish hold where the bottom makes these changes. The end of the lock wall is also twenty feet deep and an excellent place to fish.

All these big and little step-ups and walls are road signs to the fish. If you drop your bait in the fifteen-foot depth in front of the spillway, you won't entice the fish holding below the lip at seventeen feet. Small drops and scooped-out pockets in the bottom's gravel and mud will hold fish.

The natural bottom moves from season to season, depending on how much water has come over the spillway. You have to be watchful for these changes. They mean fish or no fish.

During generation a big eddy forms in front of the spillway. Drifting and jigging the eddy is a productive tactic. Dropping anchor to fish the ends of the walls is also productive. Much depends on how many generators are in operation.

Beware during times of no generation. Some areas are less than two feet below the surface and have done considerable harm to outboard props and lower units.

GAMEFISH SPECIES

Trout

Rainbows are frequently caught during generation. Local anglers say that the best time for trout is when all three generators are working. The hot spot is the left side of the powerhouse. Anglers fish from the bank on the walkway (when current allows) and do well catching rainbows.

Small spoons, spinners, jigs, and small crankbaits work well, as do nightcrawlers and minnows. Cast upstream and let your bait ride the current. Anglers push their boats up near the boils, then cast their baits and ride the current down below the launching ramps.

This technique can provide you with species other than trout. Rockfish, stripe, walleye, sauger, and catfish are also likely to hit in this area. Since the lake trout has invaded the waters below Dale Hollow Lake, you may get lucky and land one of these strong-fighting, good-tasting fish.

Rockfish

From the western launching ramp to the dam is rip-rap holding the bank in place. Rockfish get their name because they like rocks.

If you have concluded that this is a good place to look for rockfish, give yourself an A. There is less current on the eastern rip-rap, so there are fewer rockfish; but stripe love that area.

Using twenty-pound test line with a split shot ten inches above a 3/0 steel hook with a shad or large minnow on it, ride up to the swift water, cast out about twenty-five feet, and ride the current. You will have to take up slack with your reel as the water becomes shallower, but keep your bait on bottom. Large white jigs work well also.

Stripe

Stripe are almost always present below the dam. There is usually a school on the bottom near the red channel marker upstream from the eastern ramp. If you can't locate fish with a graph, you can probe this area with a minnow or a jig, Cast a minnow or one-eighth-ounce jig, and let it settle to the bottom. Work it in slowly.

If you don't have any takers, move to the end of the inside lock wall, and try there. Another good spot to try is in front of the generators. Cast into the well that is calm and work your bait into the boils. The stripe are there.

Walleye and Sauger

This is a wintertime honey hole. From November until March anglers crowd below the dam with their rods pumping jigs. Many use the three-eighths-ounce to one-ounce redhead jigs with stinger hooks and minnows. Others use lighter jigs, one-eighth-ounce, with minnows or curlytails.

The river-rig is another effective method. It is a twelve-inch section of six-pound test line with a barrel swivel on one end and a one or 1/0 hook on the other. Before you tie the rig to your main line, slide on a slip sinker, one heavy enough to keep your minnow on the bottom but as light a weight as you can. The sinker stops at the swivel, leaving your minnow free to swim.

When a fish hits, it won't feel the weight of the sinker, just the tension you have on the line. Drop your tip a few seconds so the fish can get the minnow in its mouth; then set your hook. This is a particularly good way to feel those light-biters.

You can cast the river-rig and work it back slowly, let it sit, or jig it as you drift. It is versatile and fruitful. Some anglers add a stinger hook to the river-rig.

This mess of beautiful sauger was caught below Cordell Hull Dam.

Crappie and Bluegill

These two hang out in much the same areas—in front of the spillway, along both sides of the inside lock wall, and in the quiet pocket to the right of the lock doors.

Bluegill prefer worms and crickets. Crappie like minnows and jigs.

Catfish

The technique is the same for most of the tailwaters: shad, minnows, cutbait, worms, liver, and stinkbaits fished on the bottom in the deep water in front of the powerhouse. When there is current, use more weight. Some anglers use four ounces of lead to hold their bait on the bottom. When there is little or no current, fish the deep holes.

Blue, channel, and yellow cats lie below Cordell Hull waiting for your bait. There are several structures here that catfish prefer—the whitewater in front of the turbine vents, the rip-rap on both banks, and the pockets below each ramp and against the lock wall. The giant eddy in front of the spillway gates is good for drift-fishing for cats.

The lock wall appeals to cats because with each discharge baitfish are dislodged and become easy prey. Caution must be used: the discharge can swamp a boat easily. There is a warning siren before the lock discharges its water. Your best choice is to get to the wall just after the discharge and be ready for the fish as they move back to their original holding places.

Between the east bank and the wall is a giant, slow eddy that anglers can fish from the bank. This is a good place to use dough baits while you sit and wait. Live bait is another good choice; you may pick up a stripe, crappie, bass, or sauger while you're waiting.

The water here is well oxygenated, usually has stunned or chopped up baitfish that were sucked into the turbines, offers a deep area with eddies for fish to hold in, and provides the best place to catch those fifty-pound cats. Also it is the end of the line for spawning cats in the late spring and early summer. Many of these cats stay all year in the deep holes in front of the dam and move into shallow areas at night to forage.

Catfish love to feed around the rip-rap and even take up residence in the holes among the rocks. Crawfish live here, and small fish hold in the crevices. It is an ideal feeding station.

The pockets below the launching ramps are nighttime feeding spots. These shallow backwashes are convenient areas to fish from the bank. The eddies capture food and make feeding easy.

BANK FISHING

Excellent! Several concrete steps lead to the water on both banks, and you can walk along the rip-rap below the dam. The west bank is best for trout, catfish, and rockfish. Visit the east bank for the other species.

For accomodations *see* Cordell Hull Lake chapter.

CHAPTER THIRTEEN

CENTER HILL DAM

CENTER HILL DAM IS SEVENTEEN MILES EAST of Smithville via TN 96, sixty miles from Nashville via I-40, and twenty-five miles west of Cookeville via I-40. Take the Buffalo Valley exit from I-40, turn south on TN 96, turn right at Big Rock Market, and look for the east ramp entrance on your right just up the hill from the market; then follow the signs. To get to the west ramp, continue up the hill and across the dam, then take your first right turn down the hill and right to the parking lot.

The first entrance is to the Long Branch Camp Grounds. You can put up a tent or hook up your RV here. Call 615-548-8002 for more information. The next entrance is to the west ramp. There are restrooms at this parking lot and at the top of the hill on the east side of the dam.

A "pond" below Center Hill Dam is unique in Middle Tennessee because it has several acres of surface area with easy access for anglers who fish from the bank, wade, or use a boat.

Forty-five-pound rockfish, five-plus-pound rainbow and brown trout, and seven-pound walleye have been caught here. In addition to these species, you can expect to catch stripe, sauger, bream, crappie, and largemouth and smallmouth bass.

Thanks to the TWRA's diligent stocking program, trout are abundant. The TWRA puts 125,000 rainbow and brown trout in the Caney Fork from March to November. They range in size from four inches to keepers. You will need a trout stamp to go with your fishing license in order to take trout. The rainbow trout are the main attraction for anglers, but you can enjoy a smorgasbord of species.

There are two sources of water for the pond. One is a waterfall that flows continuously on the east bank near the dam. The other is water released intermittently through the dam during periods of hydroelectric generation. At the north end of the pond is a bottleneck where the Caney Fork re-forms into a river.

Tennessee law requires persons in boats to wear life vests below dams. Look for large signs designating the zone.

While the generators are working, there is plenty of water for bass boats; their motors are needed to handle the current. You will feel more comfortable launching a bass boat from the west ramp. Lightweight canoes and boats can use either launch. The east ramp is a gradual slope into shallow water, whereas the west ramp is steeper with deeper water.

If you are using a heavy boat, you will want to get it back on your trailer soon after generation has ceased. The water level drops rapidly, and getting back to the ramp can become very difficult. There is ample water in the pond for your boat to move freely, but there isn't enough in the stream bed. If you are unable to get your boat back to the ramp before the water level drops, you can try fishing until the next period of generation when there will be plenty of water again.

Canoes and lightweight boats are ideal for high water in the pond but prove inadequate against the current during generation. When the turbines are off, these crafts can move down stream and back without difficulty.

If you go downstream on foot or in a boat, be sure you know the generation schedule. If you notice the water rising, get out quickly on the nearest bank.

You can call for the generation schedule for Center Hill Dam at 615-548-8581 or 858-4366. There is a warning device above the dam, a signboard with messages in lights, and a sound signal to let you know it is time for the turbines to start. The Corps of Engineers is evaluating an experimental safety device. If successful, these devices will be installed on other dams.

On the pond you are okay in a canoe or small boat when the turbines are turning, due to the guard wall that directs the fast water along the west bank. There are two gentle eddies outside of that swift water.

GAMEFISH SPECIES

Trout

Rainbow and brown trout are the most sought after species in the pond. The rainbows are caught more easily than browns. Danny Scott of TWRA says, "Browns become wild more quickly than rainbows and aren't as catchable. They adapt to a different diet. If you'll use a big shiner or shad or a big Countdown Rapala or a streamer on your fly rod, you'll increase your chances of catching a big brown."

Corn, salmon eggs, nightcrawlers, and minnows are favorite baits for still fishing. Little Cleos, Rooster Tails, jigs with plastic tails, and small minnow imitation lures are spinning rod favorites. Fly rodders use the Woolly Bugger more than any other fly, although others, such as scuds and the Tellico nymph, take their share.

During generation periods good-size trout are caught in the swift water and at the seams (the area between the fast and slow waters). Casting a three-way swivel with a white Rooster Tail on eighteen inches of line and a one-half-ounce casting sinker on a foot of line into the current catches trout. You can substitute large split shot for the casting sinker. The split shot will slide off the line, and instead of breaking it, you can quickly replace the weight.

Cast upstream at the ten or two o'clock position and let the weight hit bottom. Keep a tight line as the rig swings in an arc downstream. Retrieve slowly when the rig is fully downstream, and bring your lure back along the seam. Actively feeding trout will be in the current and along the seam.

Two large but gentle eddies form during generation. Casting while drifting these currents can be very productive. The baits already mentioned are effective, as are some others, including the Hot 'n' Tot Pygmy, Erie Dearie, and Wee Wart in shad color. The Pygmy and Dearie are spinner rigs for trolling nightcrawlers or minnows. The Wee Wart can be trolled or cast. Shad-colored baits interest the selective trout more because shad are abundant in the pond.

When the waters are quiet, fish the ditches and holes with live bait or casting spoons and spinners along the walls. Trolling a Woolly Bugger with a fly rod from a canoe is popular in the pond.

There are some big trout holding along the deep hole in front of the bluff on the eastern bank less than a mile downstream from

Mark Hamby of Pikeville holds a big brown trout he caught below Center Hill Dam with a homemade spoon.

the dam. You will know you are in the right place when you see a small cave in the bluff.

Anchor at the head of this hole, and let a juicy nightcrawler or minnow drift about three feet under a bobber. Let your bobber flow with the current until it is about sixty to eighty feet downstream; then reel it back slowly. Make about ten tries, then move downstream a little and do it again. Make sure you know when the next generation period will begin, and allow enough time to get back to the quiet water of the pond. You do not want to be caught down there—this is experience speaking.

Walleye

Speaking of fly rod fishing, Mike Sanderlin of Nashville's South Harpeth Outfitters caught a seven-pound walleye using a two-pound tippet. It's easier catching walleye with live bait, minnows, and nightcrawlers or with spoons and crankbaits—but not as much fun! Mike was wading and fishing at night.

The area between the east ramp and the dam is a good section for walleye, as is the end of the guard wall during generation. Trolling the Hot 'n' Tot Pygmy or Erie Dearie with crawlers or minnows or using shad imitations like the Thin Fin should connect you with a walleye.

Rockfish

Casting big lures before the sun rises during periods of generation is your best chance at these big fish. That's what Joel Martin from the nearby Big Rock Market advises after catching a forty-five-pound monster a few years ago.

Heavy spoons, live shad, Storm's Jointed ThunderStick, and Cotton Cordell's Red Fin cast into the boils are some of the best bait choices. Use heavy gear if you expect to land a big fish in this swift water. You can fish the current from a boat or the bank. When the sun rises or the current stops, so do the rockfish.

Stripe

Use the same size spoons, jigs, and spinners for stripe as you would for trout and fish the same places. The foot of the waterfall on the east bank is a hot spot, as is the water on the downstream side of the deflector wall that runs parallel to the dam. The pond is small enough that you can fish all of it in a few hours and locate the stripe.

Bass

All three bass are lumped together in this chapter because they are close together in the pond. The end of the concrete wall along the east bank above the waterfall is one of their favorite hangouts. Other places for bass are along the deflector wall, the quiet water along the guard wall, and the east bank.

Fish the pockets of deep water in ditches and holes. Crankbaits such as Rat-L-Trap, Hot 'n' Tot (not the Pygmy), Rebel, and Rapala in shad colors are good choices.

Doug Markham of Nashville has shown Slider worms to be an excellent choice. Doug pulled three bass from the same structure in five minutes using the do-nothing style of worm fishing. He was fishing downed tress above the bluff mentioned in the trout section.

Bream

Still fish or drift with worms or crickets for hand-size bluegill next to the deflector wall. This area is one of the best places to fish in the pond. You can fish this area confident that you will catch something, but the species is not always predictable.

The east bank is the other place to dunk bait for bream, especially up from the waterfalls and out about twenty feet.

Crappie

You will find crappie in the corner where the bluff meets the eastern concrete retaining wall. Often you will catch bass and bream with the crappie.

Look for deep holes and cast live bait or jigs. For crappie try Berkley's scented Power Tubes or Crappie Bait, which you form on your hook, and Mister Twister's banana-scented grubs.

BANK FISHING

Most anglers take their fish from the bank or while wading. The east bank from the boat launch ramp to the dam is a steep bluff. It is accessible when water is not being released from the dam. Just beyond the waterfall is the end of a concrete retaining wall running parallel to the bluff from the dam. This is as far as you can go on foot. It is shallow below the waterfall, but it descends quickly from there to the end of the concrete wall. This section holds bream, bass, stripe, trout, and crappie.

Local anglers catch brown trout at the foot of the waterfall by letting a minnow drift with the current. They don't use a bobber or lead and let the minnow drift on a hook. This technique works best in low light or darkness.

The waterfall is a hot spot for stripe in the spring. You should have no trouble catching stripe with minnows, curlytail jigs (white or yellow), small spoons, or spinners. The stripe are active day and night. Lights from the dam offer a little illumination for night fishing. Along the steep bank, between the waterfall and the east ramp, you can catch walleye and trout. Trout favor corn and salmon eggs while walleye prefer minnows, night crawlers, and small gold or copper colored spoons. When the water is low, you can see the deep areas that hold fish, but the fishing is better when at least one turbine is operating.

The east ramp is one of the most popular spots for catching trout with corn or salmon eggs fished on the bottom. Put two or three kernels of corn or eggs on a small hook, size twelve to eight.

Place a small split-shot four inches above the hook. Cast out and watch your line since you don't have a bobber to indicate a strike. Once your line moves, give the fish a couple of seconds to mouth the bait; then set your hook.

The river-rig or slip sinker-rig works best because the fish doesn't feel the weight. Wary fish, usually the older and larger ones, will drop the bait if they feel something unnatural.

Wading is excellent from the ramp to the bottleneck and on downstream. If you are a wader, you may appreciate insulated waders. The water is still cold even when the air temperature reaches the 90s.

Anglers start drifting Woolly Buggers on their fly rods at the bottleneck. Beginning here, at low water, you can wade downstream casting your flies with confidence you will catch a trout.

The west bank from the dam to the bottleneck is a steep incline of construction rock. This is the preferred side for angling for jumbo fish during generation. The fast water attracts rockfish and the big trout.

Anglers catch big brown trout and rockfish in fast water on chartreuse spoons and white one-half ounce jigs or larger. The fish feed here from dawn until the sun hits the water. Rockfish that weigh over forty pounds and browns over five pounds have been caught here. Fishing from the bank for these big fish requires medium to heavy equipment.

Fishing on foot from the dam to about a mile downstream will fill your day and your creel. When no generators are on, you can walk down both banks, changing sides when the banks are too steep, until you get to the bluffs on the east bank. You can go farther, but this is enough fishing either to fill your stringer or fatigue you.

For accommodations *see* Center Hill Lake chapter.

CHAPTER FOURTEEN

OLD HICKORY DAM

OLD HICKORY DAM HAS ONE LAUNCHING
ramp on the south side near the community of Rayon City. From
I-65, take the Old Hickory Boulevard exit east to Madison. Follow
TN 45 across the river bridge and turn left to stay on Old Hickory
Boulevard; turn left on Swinging Bridge Road, right on Cinder
Road, and bear to the left to go below the dam. From US 70 near
Hermitage, take TN 45 north to Old Hickory and Rayon City, turn
right on Swinging Bridge Road, and follow the signs.

To fish from the north side bank take Rockland Road from US
31E to Louise Avenue through Rockland Recreation Area and follow the signs. There is convenient fishing from a walkway close to
the powerhouse and along the rip-rap. A rocky area extends from
the end of the rip-rap down to a small creek with steps leading part
of the way down the rocks. A dirt bank is downstream from the
creek.

The south bank has several hundred feet of rip-rap beginning
at the lock down to the ramp. Below the ramp is a comfortable place
to fish. It has a gradual slant into the river with small pieces of loose
shale. You can drive down there and park during low water.

The ramp is designed for one vehicle at a time and is func-
tional during low water.

The following depth measurements were taken while one generator was working. Midchannel from the ramp is eighteen feet
deep and rises to fourteen feet, a depth maintained to the lock
gates. The channel from the ramp to the vents of the powerhouse

varies from eighteen to ten feet deep. The bottom rises to ten feet, then falls to thirty-eight feet at the powerhouse wall. When there is no generation, this incline is a good place to fish for stripe. The north bank is also a good place.

There are six spillways 270 feet wide. The depth in front of the spillways to the end of the lock wall varies from two feet to twenty-six feet. During periods of no generation you will see rocks sticking out of the water. About twenty feet in front of the spillway gates, a ledge runs parallel to the gates from the powerhouse wall to the lock wall. It is five feet deep with a downstream drop-off to fourteen feet.

The bottom is irregular, rising and falling from ten feet to twenty-six feet deep. Downstream from the spillway closest to the powerhouse are some barely submerged rocks.

This irregular bottom gives fish excellent places to stay. With a graph you can locate to deeper areas to jig for sauger.

The corner of the powerhouse is one of the best places to fish during periods of generation. The current flows to the corner and forms an eddy. Fish hold in the slack water and feed on shad that have passed through the turbines.

An eddy forms along the north bank flowing toward the powerhouse if generators at the south end of the powerhouse are working. Fishing can be very good from the walkway on the north bank if generators near the walkway are working. The resulting current encourages rockfish to the area. To land these fish requires heavy gear and line.

Stripe

Stripe, both white and yellow, abound here. Doug Markham and I, as well as the north bank anglers, were catching these little scrappers in rapid-fire succession. Doug got tired of putting on minnows and went to a small silver Dardevle. There was no letup in the action for him.

His technique was to let the lure hit bottom and to raise it slowly, then let it fall slowly. The fish took the bait on the fall most often. We would drift from a twelve-foot depth to twenty-four-foot depth in front of the quiet generators.

I used a river-rig. A hook is tied to twelve inches of line, and the other end is tied to a barrel swivel. A small egg sinker is placed on the main line from the rod tip. Then the barrel swivel is tied on. The swivel prevents line twists and is a stop for the sinker. When a fish hits the minnow or worm on the hook, lowering the rod tip allows the line to go slack, and the fish is free to carry the bait without resistance because the line slides through the sinker. When enough time has elapsed for the fish to have the bait in its mouth, any slack line is reeled in and the hook is set.

The river-rig is my favorite way to find sauger and stripe. After I locate them, I can switch to a faster fishing method such as jigging.

The rig is also very useful for finding inactive fish. Inactive or nonfeeding fish won't pursue baitfish, but they will eat any that come close to their mouths.

The river-rig is particularly effective for cold-water fishing. Fish are cold-blooded creatures and become lethargic in cold water. They can't generate heat through muscle activity; therefore, they are inactive. That's when they appreciate a slow meal coming their way.

Using the river-rig is a successful technique in the cold water from November until March when sauger and stripe are most abundant below the dam.

Crappie

Crappie come up river when the water cools in November and are caught using slow techniques; usually a minnow under a bobber works best. They hang around the lock wall and in front of the spillways where the water is not very strong. Come spring, they are very active and jigs work well. They go down river after they spawn.

Other crappie spots are Manskers Creek and Dry Creek, situated between the dam and the TN 45 Bridge. The mouths of these creeks are also good places to fish for sauger. When there is enough water for your boat, go up the creeks for bass, bream, and catfish.

You will catch blue, channel, and yellow or flathead cats below the dam. They are more active during the summer but are always present.

Catfish

Cats respond to blood bait better than about anything you can use. But as you can imagine, it is impossible to keep it on your hook in swift water. Periods with no generation or areas where there is very little current are your options for this outstanding bait.

Blood bait is made from any bird (chicken) or mammal (cow, deer). There are plenty of meat processing plants to supply you with all you need. Put half an inch of blood in a cake pan to coagulate in the refrigerator. Cut into cubes and freeze until you are ready to go fishing; refreeze any you have left.

Blood baits are for quiet waters, not the water roaring through the dam. When the current below the dam is quiet or you are fishing in an easy eddy, put your bait on a number 1 treble hook and gently lower it to the bottom. You can't cast this stuff, and it will leave your hands messy. Take a towel with you.

Dough baits are frequently used because of their appeal and price. Doughs are easy to put on your hook and stay fairly well.

Use a bait-holder treble hook from a number 1 to 6/0, depending on what size cat you are after. When you have located a honey hole such as the leading edge of a hump, a depression, or a bend in the channel, lower your bait and wait. The dough bleeds off, creating a scent trail downstream. It takes fifteen minutes for it to become fully effective. If you don't have any takers within twenty to thirty minutes, try another place.

Terry Madewell is an outdoor writer and an expert cat fisherman, and he has recommended dip baits for years. His favorite brand is Doc's Catfish Getter Dip Bait.

Dip baits come in tubs like dough baits or in jars. You have to use these dip baits in a "catfish worm." You work the "dip" inside the plastic worm's crevices and holes. Because the hook is mostly covered by the plastic worm, catfish are less likely to drop it. Then cast it and wait for Mr. Whiskers to sniff it.

There are other forms of stinkbaits to choose from, such as the sponge baits (sponge and scent), tube baits (a toothpaste tube full of thick paste which is castable, durable, and expensive), and chunk baits (grape-size chunks good for casting but slow to dissolve, better suited for trotlines).

Bass

You can catch a few largemouth and smallmouth bass below the dam, but if they're the fish you're after, David Woodward suggests trying the creeks before you get to the bridge and using Rat-L-Traps.

Consult the Cheatham Lake chapter for bass fishing because Cheatham has more and bigger largemouth bass than any lake in Middle Tennessee.

For accommodations *see* Old Hickory Lake chapter.

CHAPTER FIFTEEN

PERCY PRIEST DAM

PERCY PRIEST DAM IS A SHORT DISTANCE EAST of downtown Nashville via I-40. Take the Stewarts Ferry Pike exit and turn east on Bell Road at the first traffic light to get to the dam. From Hermitage, Mount Juliet, and points east, use the Old Hickory Boulevard exit from I-40, and turn west on Bell Road. From Bell Road you can get to either bank below the dam. Both sides have parking lots, but only the west side has restrooms.

From the Cumberland River it is 6.8 miles up the Stones River to Percy Priest Dam. There are no launching ramps on this stretch of water. In fact, to get to the dam by boat, you have to put in somewhere on Cheatham Lake. Shelby Park ramp in Nashville or below Old Hickory Dam are the nearest ramps.

There is usually too little water below the dam even to get there by boat. So why am I going on about boats going to the dam? Rockfish.

During the late winter and spring and again in the fall, there is plenty of water for boats below the dam. This draining of Priest Lake is a signal for the rockfish to leave the Cumberland and swim upstream to feast on the shad coming through the generator and floodgates and to take your big striper lures.

You can tell by the full parking lots on both sides of the Stones River when the rockfish are running. The dam has only one generator on the west side, and that is where you should try to catch a big rockfish. The stream sides are elbow to elbow with anglers casting their heavy-duty rods. It's like a big picnic. Sometimes going by boat is the only way you are sure to have room to cast. Because the river is narrow, courtesy to fellow anglers is typically exercised.

Storm's Jointed ThunderStick, Cordell Cotton's Red Fin, heavy white jigs with white trailers and big shiners, or shad take many of these big fish each year. Some anglers leave without a fish and not because they didn't get a strike—they just couldn't land it once they hooked it. Go prepared for forty-pound fish. Tackle made for that size fish will hold a fifty pounder should you get lucky.

Crappie, catfish, bream, bass, sauger, walleye, and stripe also come up during the high water. Most of the year they can be found somewhere along that 6.8 miles down to the Cumberland River.

During low water periods, the tailwaters get very low, exposing the ridges in the channel's gravel floor. There is no fish action then, but you can walk downstream and fish the holes at the bridge and downstream. The farther down you go, the more water and fish are available.

David Woodward of Nashville won't let me tell you where his honey hole is, but he agreed to let me tell you that it can be reached by walking. During low water, David has caught all the species mentioned earlier. I was impressed with his crappie and walleye catches.

Canoes and john boats are just the ticket for low-water fishing. There are some "bassy places" close to the US 70 Bridge. Taking a day to fish down to the Cumberland and back should be rewarding since there is very little fishing pressure on this stream. Check the generation schedule before you go (615-883-2351).

Wading is another option for fishing below the dam. As with wading below all dams, be cautious. Pay attention to any change in the water level, and if it begins to rise, get out on the nearest bank quickly.

There are some deep holes, too deep for wading but just right for belly-boating. A belly-boat and a fly rod will get you a lot of fun.

For accommodations see Percy Priest Lake chapter.

For a list of phone numbers for dam generation schedules and lake conditions, see Appendix A.

CHAPTER SIXTEEN

CHEATHAM DAM

BETWEEN ASHLAND CITY AND CLARKSVILLE on TN 12, at the community of Cheap Hill, is Dam Road leading to Cheatham Dam and the boat ramp. If you prefer a scenic drive along the river from Ashland City, turn left after you cross Marks Creek Bridge on to Chapmansboro Road. Turn right after crossing the Sycamore Creek Bridge. You will see a launching ramp on your left below the bridge. The distance by this route is the same as staying on TN 12, but you don't encounter the steep hill-and-valley driving. It's a level drive with one hill to climb to rejoin TN 12.

There isn't a ramp on the southwestern side of the river, but the bank fishing is better than on the other side because you have a longer bank to fish. You get there by turning north off TN 49, east of Ashland City, on Old Lock Road, then on Miller Chapel Road. If you are coming from Dickson or Charlotte on TN 49, turn north on Bowker Road, then on Miller Chapel Road. There is a baitshop before you get to the dam on Miller Chapel Road.

I love fishing below dams, and Cheatham is one of my two favorites, Center Hill being the other. Unlike lakes with wide expanses to fish, I like the structure and confinement below dams.

Fish seem more willing to take your bait when at least one turbine is working and creating a little current. The weather, seasons, water conditions, and an angler's attitude are also important factors.

The day I took the following measurements, there had been no generation for four hours and the water was very low. Low water can cause you problems launching and navigating. (Remember when you go below Cheatham Dam, these depth readings will be relative. If you find the lock depth eighteen feet deep rather than fourteen feet deep, add four feet to the depths in this chapter.)

Direct your boat down the river side of the ramp during low water because the water is deeper there and it's easier to unload. Since there is no current, you don't have to worry about your boat getting away from you.

During low water, once you are under power, move your boat to midchannel where it is fifteen feet deep. Aim for the lock, and the water will not be less than fourteen feet deep along this path. The end of the left lock wall is about one hundred yards from the dam. The depth is irregular along this wall into the lock and varies from ten to fourteen feet deep.

The back left and right corners of the lock are thirteen feet deep and outstanding places to catch crappie, sauger, stripe, and catfish. They aren't always there at the same time, but sometimes you can get all four species within an hour. You can usually catch stripe and sauger in the same places.

Inside the lock the average depth is fourteen feet with little mounds and depressions. The lock is almost always productive. The end of the right lock wall is very fruitful during periods of generation. It drops from ten feet deep at the base of the wall to seventeen feet deep a few yards downstream. Drifting and bumping jigs off the bottom along this uneven incline can result in your catching larger sauger than are usually found in the lock.

The seven spillway gates extend 480 feet from the lock wall to the powerhouse wall. In the large area below the gates, you will find enormous differences in the bottom's topography. Your motor will hit rocks during low water periods. Once you've cleared the rocks, the bottom may drop off to eighteen feet deep. This is wonderful structure. To the four species mentioned, add rockfish, bream, bass, gar, and carp. All these fish inhabit a relatively small area, which is what thrills me about fishing below the Cumberland River dams.

Immediately below the seven spillways is a ten-foot depression that runs from the lock wall to the powerhouse. Downstream about fifteen feet is a ledge ranging in depth from three feet to nine feet, running parallel to the spillways. This ledge may have been uniform when first made, but since then it has suffered from erosion and beatings from floods. The ledge lines up with the jut out in the lock wall.

Below this ledge, the irregular bottom varies from ten to fifteen feet deep. It is deeper near the lock. The bottom of the ledge is a migration route for fish and rarely fails to produce.

At the corner of the powerhouse wall the water is nine feet deep. Just around the corner in front of the generator vents, it is forty-four feet deep. This corner is a prized place. A rope has been attached to the wall where one boat can moor during generation and catch rockfish, sauger, stripe, and catfish.

The bottom rises sharply from forty-four feet to seven feet or less in front of the generator vents. Rocks are visible during low water. There is a line of rocks across this shallow part of the river, and you can see the riffles and turbulence when water is flowing.

Anglers run up to the boils, drop their bait, and drift downstream for rockfish. Some use lead to keep the bait on the bottom, and others use none or very little. They drift for more than one hundred yards, then drive back to the boils and do it again. Some anglers anchor on the seam of the swift water and use heavy jigs or weights to keep their bait on the bottom where the big fish hold. It's a good idea to use "disposable" anchors here. Anchors often wedge among the rocks and become part of the bottom. In low water you can see the floating frayed ends of ropes.

Walleye seem to like the current along the southwest bank. Bank anglers catch walleyes, sauger, cats, rockfish, and stripe from near the powerhouse downstream to the end of the rip-rap and beyond. This long bank is easily accessible by steps or walking over the rip-rap. There are excellent opportunities for bank anglers on both banks. More bank is available to fish from on the southwestern side because the lock wall takes up about the first one hundred yards of the northeastern bank.

The techniques I suggest for fishing here are as described in other chapters—jigging, live minnows on river-rigs, casting and trolling spinners, and small spoons. Use live shad or cutbait for stripers and catfish alike. Drift with the current or anchor at the edge of the current for rockfish, and anchor and fish on bottom for catfish. There are fifty-pound cats here and forty-pound stripers.

From November until April is my favorite time below the dam. Sauger, stripe, crappie, and a few walleye are biting then. The lock and the left third of the spillway area along the lock wall are where most of these fish are caught. Stripers are in the current below the powerhouse.

Downstream creeks prove fruitful to fruitless, depending on the generation schedule. When there is current to fill the creeks, stripe, crappie, and bass will bite. The creek mouths are usually better for sauger, stripe, and small stripers.

Crappie hold among the downed trees in the Cumberland River, and in the spring you have to be there early to get a tree to fish. They hold in the eddies caused by the trees, out of the full current. Use heavy line and light wire hooks to keep from having to retie your tackle, because you will get snagged.

Summer angling below Cheatham Dam yields predominantly catfish (all the time) and stripers (in the current during periods of generation). You can catch the other species mentioned earlier, but they aren't as concentrated in the summer as the rest of the year.

Bass anglers catch spotted bass, smallies, and bucketmouths on the river. Spots and smallies like the rip-rap and river banks. In calmer waters, largemouth hold in the creeks and in cuts in the bank. Drifting and casting crankbaits and spinnerbaits works best. The area above the dam has remarkable largemouth angling (*see* Cheatham Lake chapter for more information).

Now for the best tip in this chapter. My friend David Woodward and I discovered that to catch big stripe, those weighing a pound or more, you have to fish the high clay banks on the outside bend of the river when the current is strong. We found that one-eighth- and one-fourth-ounce, white or chartreuse jigs cast at a 45-degree angle upstream to the waterline and worked downstream on the drop-off produced smashing hits. Stripe wouldn't take our bait if it was offered at any other angle.

David and I would start at the first outside bend on the northeast bank and work that bank for five miles drifting in the current. We picked up stripe by casting in front of logs, letting the current sweep the jig under them where the fish were holding, but most of our big stripe came from banks with no visible cover.

FACILITIES

Baitshop and Fishing Supplies
   Crotty's Baitshop, on Dam Road about a mile before you get to the Cumberland. Pat Crotty opens about 6:00 A.M.; when the fish are really biting, she opens earlier. You can get bait, beverages, snacks, and sandwiches (615-792-7933).
   For accommodations *see* Cheatham Lake chapter.

CHAPTER SEVENTEEN

NORMANDY DAM AND THE DUCK RIVER

NORMANDY LAKE IS THE SMALLEST LAKE described in this book, and the dam has the smallest spillway, but it has big saugeye. Walleye and sauger sometimes mate naturally, but the majority are produced in hatcheries for stocking lakes and streams. Such is the case with these saugeye.

They were stocked in Normandy Lake but were carried through the dam during high-water conditions on the lake. Doug Pelren, TWRA fisheries biologist, says saugeye stack up during the winter in front of the dam and are carried downstream during periods of discharge. These sterile fish won't reproduce, but they will get to be a good-size fish. In 1991 many weighed between five and eight pounds.

The Duck River below the dam is stocked with rainbow and brown trout. Five hundred muskies were stocked in 1991. These eight- to ten-inch fish were released over a hundred-mile stretch of the Duck from Marshall County through Maury County and into Hickman County. Muskie stocking will continue through 1993.

In a few years, when they reach the legal limit of thirty inches, you will have a whale of a fight landing one of these vicious critters. Be careful of their teeth; use pliers to dislodge your hook.

I've had two experiences catching these strong fish. They have chewed and twisted my plugs beyond belief. They fight as hard out of the water as they do in it. My friend Paul Carpenter of Rochester,

Minnesota, got one into our canoe only to have the muskie get loose and knock everything overboard. Be careful! 'Nuff said.

The Duck River has hardly become a good-size stream before it runs into the Normandy Lake basin. When it is released as a stream again, it has gained in size. Its waters now flow cold from the bottom of Normandy, just right for trout and saugeye.

It is also a well-known catfish stream to the locals. Finding the catfish holes requires finding pools downstream from the dam.

The bottom is rock and gravel with high banks of construction rock for about 200 feet down from the dam on both sides of the stream. Then the bank is low and level on the eastern (parking lot) side. The west bank is rock for one hundred yards or more, then levels off. Both banks have trees downstream from the bridge. It is excellent for wading or bank fishing, also good for canoeing. There are some shallow spots that canoeists will have to negotiate during low water, but nothing difficult.

During periods of low flow from the dam, the water at the lip of the spillway is six feet deep. There is an eddy at the two walls in front of the spillway; the larger eddy is on the east side. This slow-moving eddy has a depth of ten feet. The stronger current moves toward the far bank that is accessible by walking from the bridge or wading across the stream.

Because the water is cold, there is good fishing here during the summer. In the spring and during the fall draw-down, the fishing is better because the high water entices more and bigger fish to the area.

Barton Springs Campgrounds is less than two miles east of the dam on Normandy Road. It offers easy access to the lake as well. There is a convenient baitshop/grocery store about a mile west of the dam.

To get to the dam from Shelbyville, go east on US Alt 41, then turn east on Normandy Road. Cross the railroad tracks and turn left in the town of Normandy. The dam is about two miles.

From north of Manchester, turn off US 41 on Bashaw Creek Road to Blanton Chapel, follow Blanton Chapel Road, and turn on Hiles Road (Bell Road on some maps). When you cross the bridge over Normandy Lake, turn right. The dam is less than two miles on your right.

From Tullahoma take TN 269 off US Alt 41 north of the city. This road takes you through the town of Normandy to the dam.

For those traveling down from Normandy Dam by canoe, it is

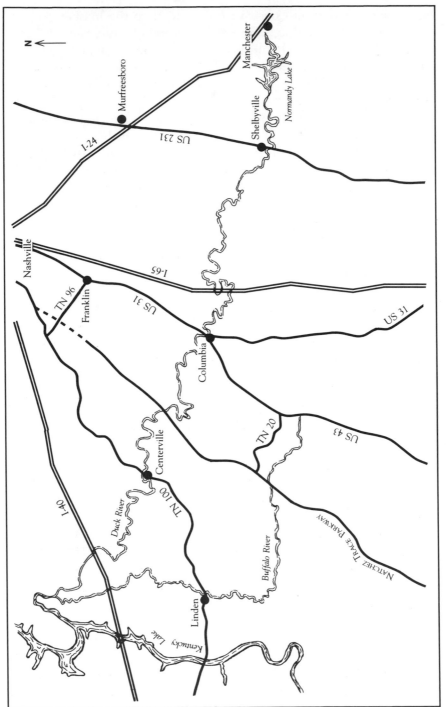

Map Fourteen: The Duck River

248.5 miles to the mouth of the Duck where it joins the Tennessee River, a few miles east of New Johnsonville on US 70 (*see* Big Bottoms chapter). Although the Buffalo is favored as a canoe stream, the Duck has a lot to offer to anglers.

In addition to the four species mentioned, it has smallmouth, largemouth, and Kentucky bass, bream, crappie and stripe. The mouth of the Duck is one of the top wintertime hot spots for sauger.

The Duck has one commercial canoe rental company (see below). Locating other access points requires asking permission of land owners. A rule of thumb is to look for access areas near bridges. There are more than two dozen bridges between the dam and the mouth. Most of these places are also good for bank fishing.

FACILITIES

Canoe Rental

Forest Landing Canoe Livery, Highway 31A, Chapel Hill, TN 37034 (615-364-7874). Canoes, campground, store.

Campgrounds

Henry Horton State Park, PO Box 128, Chapel Hill, TN 37034 (615-364-2222). Camping, cabins, inn, restaurant, swimming pool, other forms of recreation.

For additional accommodations *see* Normandy Lake chapter.

CHAPTER EIGHTEEN

TIMS FORD DAM AND ELK RIVER

BEFORE THE ELK RIVER IS SET FREE TO JOIN the Tennessee River, it flows through Woods Reservoir, then through Tims Ford Lake. It comes out of Tims in a peculiar manner.

A big channel runs straight down from the dam where it is joined by a large concrete spillway that curves from the dam into the main channel like a big reversed C. The Elk River swings even wider. It flows from the eastern side of the dam and enters the main channel farther downstream than the spillway junction, just above the TN 50 bridge.

GAMEFISH SPECIES

Catfish

The water immediately in front of the dam is sometimes quiet and a haven for catfish. Channel and yellow cats are present. During periods of generation, it becomes a good place to fish for all species, especially trout.

Trout

Rainbow and brown trout are in the cold water that flows from the side of the dam. The first hundred-yard stretch of this stream below the dam has a good deal of brush and may be hard to fish. Around the bridge is easier, but if you like a challenge, you may find fish few anglers have approached. From the dam downstream for

Striper guide Jim McClain of Winchester knows where to hook 'em on Tims Ford.

fourteen miles is a stretch considered a cold-water fishery suitable for trout.

Walleye

Walleye up to ten pounds are caught below the dam, but most run between two and four pounds. The best times to catch walleye are during high water in the winter and spring.

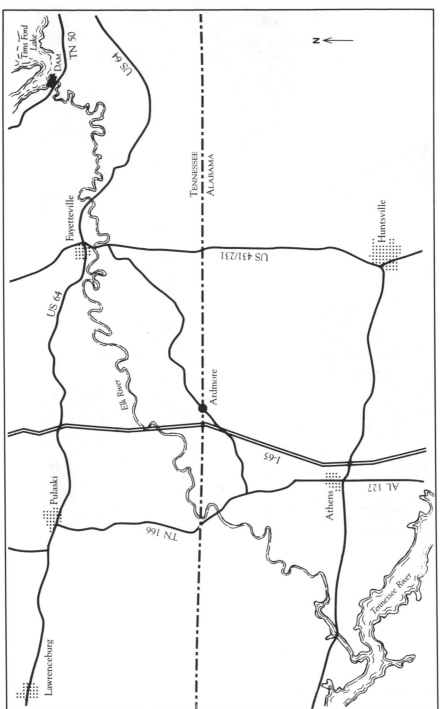

Map Fifteen: The Elk River

Rockfish

Since the spring flood of 1991, rockfish are below the dam and have been caught as far downstream as Fayetteville.

BANK FISHING

High rock banks near the dam give way to fishable banks and gravel bars near the bridge. Canoes and john boats can float comfortably in the stream, and bank anglers also have excellent access.

There is parking on the east side of the TN 50 bridge. For a good view of the complex area below the dam, drive to the top of the dam for a look. Stop also at the overlook for a view of the large curved concrete spillway.

The Elk runs about 220 miles from its headwaters to its mouth, with 180 miles of the stream in Tennessee. It enters Alabama due south of Pulaski. Tims Ford Dam is at about river-mile 133, leaving close to 100 miles of river between the dam and Alabama.

Below Tims Ford Dam during nongeneration periods, the Elk is shallow with a gravel bottom and easy current—excellent conditions for wading and waving a fly rod for trout. It's about fifty feet wide with gravel bars making easy access for canoeists. There are twenty bridges with varying ease of access along this hundred-mile section.

It's about forty miles downstream to Fayetteville, and the Elk broadens to about sixty-five feet but is still a peaceful stream with easy canoeing: Class I. By the time it passes Elkton, another forty miles, the Elk is a few feet wider and still gentle. The entire route is scenic with beautiful changes from high, steep, rocky bluffs to flat, tilled lowlands and tree-lined banks. From Elkton it is about twenty miles to Alabama.

FACILITIES

Elk River Canoe Rental. Route 1, Box 20, Kelso, TN 37348 (615-937-6886) or Route 2, Box 77, Flintville, TN 37335 (615-937-6886). Primitive camping on river, restrooms, trips ranging from a few hours to several days, bass and trout fishing on Elk River.

For additional accommodations *see* Tims Ford Lake chapter.

Cathy Summerlin's keeper trout taken on a nightcrawler from the Caney Fork River.

PART THREE

STREAM FISHING

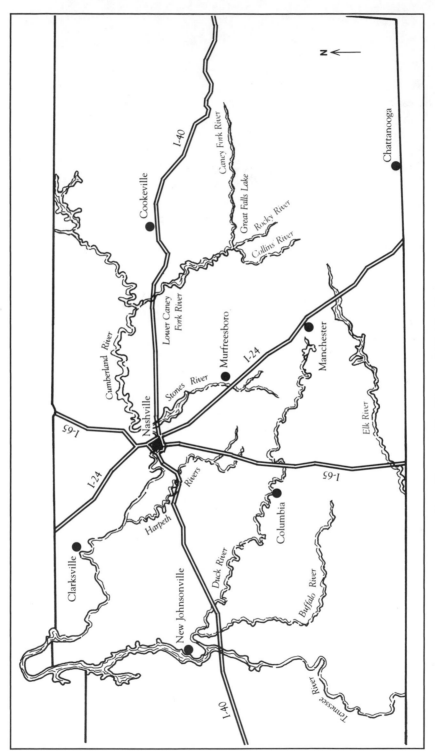

Map Sixteen: The Rivers of Middle Tennessee

THE STREAMS

MORE THAN A DOZEN STREAMS ARE INCLUDED
in the five following chapters. Many important but small tributaries
that offer you good fishing opportunities have been incorporated
into the appropriate chapters. For instance, the chapter on Great
Falls Lake is about three rivers and nine tributaries rather than a
lake.

You can legally travel on any of Tennessee's navigable streams.
The sticky part is legally defining a navigable stream. There is no
question, however, that landowners own their banks, and you are
trespassing if you set foot there.

Two rules of thumb will make your stream fishing more pleasant. Get permission to be on private property and use public lands.
Public lands include road right-of-ways and bridges. Most of the
access points in these chapters are at bridges.

If you are granted the privilege to use private lands, honor the
landowner's trust. Keep your litter; better yet, take home litter that
you find. Don't harm fields and crops with automobiles and fires;
close the gates you open; and, in general, behave as a thoughtful
guest—because you are a guest.

Stream widths vary from a few feet to more than a hundred,
and of course their depths will vary. Current is another factor to
consider when going fishing. Larger streams, especially when their
mouths empty into a lake, contain many more species. Small
streams usually contain largemouth and smallmouth bass, rock bass,
bream, and rough fish, such as carp, suckers, and baitfish.

The smaller wading streams restrict your options and make
fishing easier. The banks are closer, structure is easily visible, and
deep holes are usually obvious. You fish the available water and
move on.

Your lure selection is restricted to small lures appropriate for smaller stream fish. I'm not saying you can't catch a five-pound largemouth from a small stream—it's been done too often. But under normal situations, a two-pound fish is about tops, and that's what you should go prepared to catch.

Light lines, two- to four-pound test, are in order. A five-foot ultralight rod with an ultralight reel rounds out a stream outfit. The short rod is maneuverable in tight places, and it is capable of landing twenty-pound fish. Rarely will you need the hundred yards of line a small reel holds, except with a twenty-pound fish.

Because you can reach most of the snags you may hang on, you don't need to carry a big tackle box to replace lost lures. One or two small boxes, such as Plano's 3598 Phantom Tackle Mate or the 3213 Mini-Magnum, will slip comfortably into a pocket.

Comfort is important while you are wading a stream, and the heaviest thing you want to carry is your fish.

Canoe fishing is my favorite system. Canoes go anywhere bass boats go and many places they can't. They are easy to transport to streams and easy to park when I want to do some wading or bank fishing. I have fished many of the streams in the next few chapters from a canoe. Try it. You'll like it.

CHAPTER NINETEEN

LOWER CANEY FORK RIVER

THE TWENTY-SEVEN-MILE WATERWAY FROM Center Hill Dam to Carthage offers the river tripper a variety of fishing experiences. Canoeing and fishing the lower Caney Fork River's cold water is a cornucopia of long, smooth, flat runs to the short, rocky drops where the current rushes white. There are places where trout, rockfish, walleye, stripe, bream, smallmouth, and largemouth bass wait.

Go prepared to catch them all. Take light to medium tackle for all species except the rockfish. Rockfish over forty pounds have been taken from the Caney Fork.

CANOEING THE CANEY FORK

A three-day trip breaks the canoe trek into eight- to ten-mile segments without your having to strain at the paddle. It can be done in a weekend for those not wanting to take time to fish for their supper and still enjoy a long canoe ride. Of course there are shorter trips you can manage in a few hours.

Your trip down the Caney Fork should start with planning. You can arrange for Big Rock Market to supply you with a canoe and pick-up service or arrange transportation with canoeing partners by leaving one vehicle at your take-out point and taking another to your put-in area.

Deciding how long your trip will last and how much food and

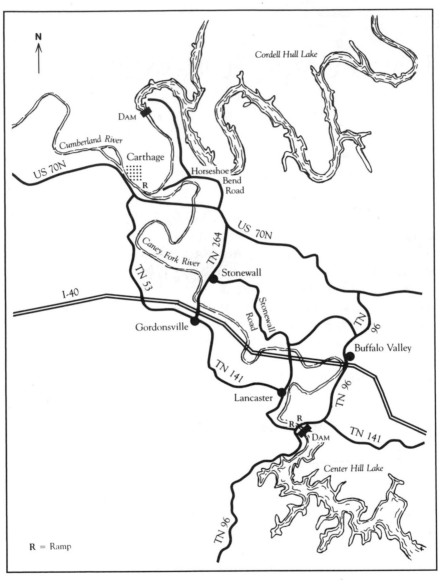

N

Cordell Hull Lake

DAM

Cumberland River

US 70N

Carthage

R

Horseshoe
Bend
Road

US 70N

Caney Fork River

TN 264

TN 53

Stonewall

I-40

Stonewall
Road

Gordonsville

TN 96

Buffalo Valley

TN 141

Lancaster

TN 96

R
R
DAM

TN 141

Center Hill Lake

TN 96

R = Ramp

Map Seventeen: Lower Caney Fork River

water you should carry are your first considerations. Although there are no convenience stores on the banks of the Caney Fork, there is one place where you can walk up steps cut into the steep bank and across the road to a market. This is in Lancaster, three miles by water from the dam. This could also be your take-out point on a short trip.

The next take-out is Happy Hollow, about five miles from the dam. There is good walleye fishing above and below the Happy Hollow gravel bar. The area is marked with signs on TN 96 between the I-40 exit at Buffalo Valley and the Big Rock Market where you turn to go to the dam.

A bit over six miles downstream from the dam is an unofficial canoe access at one of Tennessee's official rest stops for I-40 travelers. You will recognize the area from the water by passing under the first I-40 bridge. There are five interstate bridges in the first twelve miles of river.

Nine miles downstream is Bettys Bend and Laycock's Bridge. This old iron bridge high over the river gives many of those driving over it the "willies." It has the old-fashioned board runners for your tires. The view from the bridge is spectacular when the fog is rising off the river.

Beyond Bettys Bend is the fourth interstate bridge and the beginning of Betty's Island. You can canoe down either side of the island; the right side is faster and shorter.

At the end of the island is the mouth of Smith Fork Creek, reported to be the best spot to catch supper. You can catch walleye, trout, rockfish, stripe, and bass within fifty yards of the train trestle.

Camping along the Caney Fork should be arranged with landowners. *Warning:* do not camp where water can reach during periods of generation. Picking up more litter than your own makes it easier for later canoeists to get permission to stay. Be courteous to the environment—it's someone's backyard.

On the second day of your trip you will notice some changes in the river. There are longer straight stretches and a gravel bottom with a lazy flow. You should be aware that the Caney Fork's flow varies. When there is partial generation at the dam, you will float along easily. When there is full generation, you will be carried along swiftly. The farther you are from the dam, the less you will notice the effect.

The next take-out is at mile sixteen on the right bank under the Gordonsville Bridge, two miles from the Gordonsville community. By road, it is a few miles from the Gordonsville–Carthage exit from I-40.

You can drive below the northeast end of the bridge if you want to use this as a put-in or take-out area. I've had rockfish break my line while I was fishing here. Dawn and dusk are the best times to catch them with spoons and crankbaits.

Before you reach the next take-out, four miles downstream at the twenty-mile point, is Dripping Rock Bluff. This scenic bluff has spring water falling from ferns growing in the cracks of the cliff. Don't let the occasional deep underground rumbles frighten you. I do not know the reason for these noises, but I have heard them on every visit.

The US 70N Bridge is a mile farther. There is a fair place to take out on the right bank before you reach the bridge. A little bank climbing is required, but there is a road off US 70N leading to the take-out spot. Just beyond the bridge on the left you can see the home of former Tennessee Senator Albert Gore, Sr., overlooking the Caney Fork River.

The next four-mile run takes you along the last bend of your trip. This is a scenic arc below high bluffs. Hawks nest here, and during late June and July you will probably see the fledglings soar and hear their high-pitched screams. Crappie, rockfish, trout, smallmouth bass, and stripe are the primary species in this section.

Once around the bend, you will see the Cumberland River. The Caney Fork becomes lazier in its last few miles because the Cumberland acts like a dam holding the water back. From the mouth of the Caney Fork, you will paddle across the Cumberland to the north shore and the last stop in your twenty-eight-mile odyssey. There is a ramp for easy access, just like the one at the beginning of your trip back at Center Hill Dam.

The mouth of the Caney Fork is worth fishing. Bigger rockfish hang around the point and down the underwater ledge formed by the Caney Fork. Trout are caught here also. Bass and crappie are along the south bank at the junction. But if you have been fishing all the way downstream, you probably have caught all the fish you want.

John Binkley of Hermitage and I met in canoes one foggy morning. After we talked a while, he handed me a lure saying, "If you aren't using a 'brown boy' you aren't catching all the fish you could be catching!" He and his friend Andy Mizell spent years searching for *the* Caney Fork lure. Brown boy is a brown one-eighth-ounce Rooster Tail. I thanked John for the lure after trying to persuade him I had other spinners. He replied, "But you don't have a brown boy."

I tied the spinner on, and he was right. I began catching more fish. Trout, bass, rockfish, and stripe were boated and released within an hour of fishing with it. It was the only lure I used for the rest of my trip. Thanks, John.

BANK FISHING

You can fish from the bank in many places. With a map you can find easy-access areas by road. The I-40 rest area is a good and easy spot to fish. A hot spot at the junction of Smith Fork Creek, also called Sebowisha, is a long walk from the interstate, according to some anglers I met while canoeing. With a map you can see where to get closer and park legally (which you can't do on the interstate) by taking Helm Road between Gordonsville and Lancaster.

If you are fishing below the dam and the generators begin, you can drive to Happy Hollow and have about one and one-half hours of fishing before the water arrives. There is another one and one-half hours before the water arrives at Betty's Island. It's one more hour before the water at Gordonsville Bridge begins to rise. If you leave the dam and go directly to Gordonsville Bridge, you should have close to four more hours of fishing.

FACILITIES

Canoe Service and Supplies

Big Rock Market. Route 1, Silver Point, TN 38582 (615-858-9942). Canoe service, deli, groceries, fishing license, excellent selection of fishing supplies. Don't forget to ask for fishing information and a generation schedule. On TN 96 near Center Hill Dam. Take Buffalo Valley exit #268 from I-40; market is five miles on right at stop sign.

For camping and other accommodations, see Center Hill Lake chapter.

For phone numbers and generation schedules, see Appendix A.

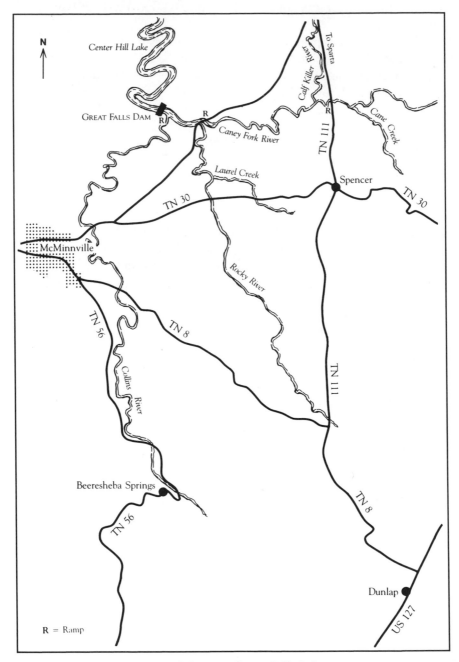

N

Center Hill Lake

GREAT FALLS DAM

R

R

Caney Fork River

Laurel Creek

Calf Killer River

To Sparta

R

Cane Creek

TN 111

Spencer

TN 30

TN 30

McMinnville

Rocky River

TN 56

TN 8

TN 111

Collins River

TN 8

Beeresheba Springs

TN 56

Dunlap

US 127

R = Ramp

Map Eighteen: Great Falls Lake

CHAPTER TWENTY

GREAT FALLS LAKE

THE UPPER CANEY FORK RIVER AND THE Rocky River join two miles above Great Falls Dam. The Collins River joins them just above the dam. Together they form Great Falls Lake. Below the dam is Center Hill Lake. Since these are three distinct waterways, we will look at them individually.

UPPER CANEY FORK RIVER

The upper Caney Fork River has two sections. From its origin near Campbell Junction in Cumberland County to the community of Dodson in south-central White County, it is a small stream. The section from Dodson to Great Falls Dam becomes a wider, navigable river. South of Sparta under the TN 111 Bridge is a launching ramp. It's about fifteen miles downstream from TN 111 to Great Falls Dam. Bass and crappie are the main attractions, but you can catch trout, bream, and muskie.

The width of this section ranges from 80 feet to over 150 feet farther down river. Average depth is eight feet. You can catch trout, smallmouth and largemouth bass, rock bass, and bream.

Canoeing the Caney Fork makes an excellent trip. You can put in at Dodson and take out at any of six bridges downstream. There are other take-out areas where roads come close to the Caney Fork. The river is Class I below Dodson and is suitable for beginning canoeists.

You can reach a good little trout stream by canoeing from the bridge upstream about a mile and turning right into Cane Creek. Cane Creek is fifteen miles long with an average width of thirty-five feet. In addition to trout, it has smallmouh and rock bass. This creek, like many in the area, is stocked by TWRA with rainbow and brown trout.

Calfkiller, another of these trout streams, joins the Caney Fork about a mile below the TN 111 Bridge. It is about thirty miles long and averages thirty-five feet in width and six feet in depth. It contains the same species as Cane Creek plus channel catfish. Calfkiller is easily canoeable from Sparta to the Caney Fork. It is navigable farther upstream from Sparta during the rainy season, but the river wiggles like a tortured snake.

ROCKY RIVER

The Rocky River is an excellent trout stream. The best trout action is at the mouth of Laurel Creek upstream to above White Hill. Smallies, largemouth, and crappie are prevalent near the mouth with muskie, bream, and rock bass found here, too. You can use a motorboat from the mouth of the Rocky River upstream about five miles to the mouth of Laurel Creek during summer pool. A canoe will serve you better farther up. The Rocky is twenty miles long with an average depth of three feet.

Laurel Creek, a ten-mile-long trout stream with a three-foot depth, is fair for canoeing. It joins the Rocky River due east of Spencer. There is no launching ramp on the Rocky.

COLLINS RIVER

The boat launching ramp on the Collins River is King's ramp off TN 287, a couple of miles upstream from the mouth. There is backwater from the junction with the Caney Fork to above the Hennessee Bridge on TN 288. Above this point you will need a canoe.

Many canoeists put in at Mount Olive near the Grundy–Warren County line and paddle to the Hennessee Bridge on

While canoeing, Maria Summerlin caught one of Tennessee's most plentiful fish, the bluegill.

TN 288. This is a forty-one-mile trip. It's another eight miles from the bridge to the mouth. Trout are in the headwaters and feeder creeks down to Irving College. The same species predominant in the Caney Fork and Rocky Rivers are in the Collins, including muskie.

The following are trout streams:

- White County—Calfkiller Creek and Caney Fork River.
- Van Buren County—Cane Creek, Laurel Creek, and Rocky River.
- Warren County—Mountain Creek, Charles Creek, Hills Creek, Taylor Creek, North Prong of Barren Fork River, Barren Fork River, and Collins River.

Fish the structures we've discussed in previous chapters while angling in these streams. Trout like places where you normally find smallmouth bass. A species of fish behave much the same from one body of water to the next, so apply what you learned in the Lower Caney Fork River chapter.

No matter the species, the biggest fish move into the best feeding areas. If that fish is removed, it is usually a matter of minutes before another large fish takes that spot. That's why you can keep returning to places you've caught fish and catch more.

Not only are the streams mentioned here worth fishing, but many of their smaller feeder creeks are too. A stream doesn't have to be listed or written about to hold trout. They swim to comfortable waters where there is food. That can be in any of the small creeks measuring only a few inches deep and many miles from where they were stocked.

CHAPTER TWENTY-ONE

THE HARPETH RIVERS

THERE ARE FOUR HARPETH RIVERS IN TEN-
nessee, they converge near the Pasquo–Bellevue area before their waters empty into the Cumberland River a few miles above Cheatham
Dam.

The Big Harpeth originates near College Grove where several
creeks merge in the space of a few miles. The West Harpeth begins
in the community of West Harpeth, south of Franklin, and is joined
by Leipers Fork Creek before crossing under TN 96 bridge. Four
miles downstream on the north side of Del Rio Pike, the Big and
West Harpeths join waters.

The Little Harpeth starts southeast of Brentwood and blends
with the Big Harpeth at the US 100 bridge between Pasquo and
Bellevue.

The South Harpeth springs up between Leipers Fork and
Craigfield off Pinewood Road. It runs through Fernvale and joins
the other waters near I-40 south of Pegram.

The Harpeth has over one hundred miles of Class I canoeing
with a few Class II rapids. It is a state scenic river offering a wide
variety of fish, including bass, bream, catfish, crappie, stripe, rockfish, and sauger.

Bank fishing and wading are easy in many areas. Be sure to get
the landowner's permission before trespassing or camping. Most of
the landowners along the South Harpeth have banned fishing on
their property. It seems that trespassing anglers damaged or littered
their land. Too bad—the South Harpeth is an excellent smallmouth fishery.

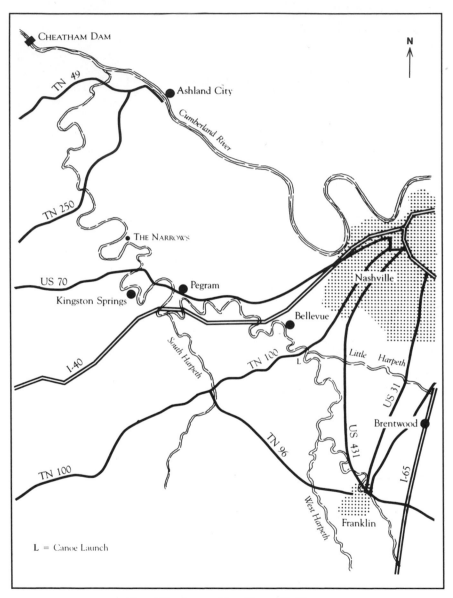

Map Nineteen: The Harpeth Rivers

Canoeing or floating a john boat is another good way to enjoy these streams. Let's look at access points for canoeists. You can put in on the West Harpeth at the Old 96 Bridge and float to the next access at the New 96 Bridge, a distance of six river miles. An additional four miles takes you to the Big Harpeth. Eleven river miles bring you to the next take-out on Old Natchez Trace.

You can put in on the Big Harpeth in Franklin at Pinkerton Park and float six miles to the US 431 bridge north of town. From the bridge to the Old Natchez Trace access is thirteen miles.

These stretches offer catfish, bream, and bass. The water is shallow in the summer with riffles; you will have to push or pull your craft across them. Fish the deep pools between riffles and cast spinnerbaits to the undercut banks for bass.

Flipping a fly rod with a popping bug is fun for taking bluegill, sunfish, warmouth, and rock bass. Catfish hide in deep pools and eddies behind the riffles and fallen trees.

The canoe access at the US 100 bridge is ten miles downstream from the Old Natchez Trace access, then three miles to the Old Harding Road bridge. From Old Harding Road it is 6.5 miles to the historic Newsome Mill built in 1862. Smallmouth, largemouth, and rock bass are the main game fish in this stretch. Catfish and bream live in the entire system.

It's a short two-mile paddle to the next access point east of Pegram on US 70, then four miles into Pegram. The next trek is to Shacklett, about five miles, then another five miles to The Narrows. This float will take you through some wonderful smallmouth waters . . . with more to come.

The five mile loop of the Narrows puts you within 200 feet of where you began this section. This is a nice lazy float on a summer afternoon. There may be some portaging over a few riffles during low water.

Below the bridge at The Narrows there are two more access points at other bridges. The first bridge on Cedar Hill Road is a little over two miles, and the last bridge on Claylick Road is seven miles beyond that.

From Claylick Road bridge there is a twelve-mile run of the Harpeth to the TN 49 bridge and the Harpeth River Recreation Area. This last twelve miles has some of the best angling the river offers, and add to that two miles down to the mouth and Dozier's Dock on the Cumberland River.

Motorboats can put in at the recreation area and move upstream several miles. Ray Dozier, owner of Dozier's Dock and Restaurant, caught a bass that lacked one ounce of being ten pounds out his front door in the mouth of the Harpeth.

The river has good structure from the mouth upstream several miles with log-strewn flats, deadfalls along the brushy, undercut banks, deep pockets in the channel, and steep bluffs with drop-offs into the channel.

From February to April many species head up the Harpeth to spawn—rockfish, stripe, sauger, and crappie. Only the rockfish doesn't reproduce. Sauger and stripe will seek moving water, usually at the junction of the Harpeth and feeder creeks. Crappie head for the brush and deadfalls in calm, shallow water.

Toward the end of March, smallies start to move on their beds and are in peak spawn during April and May. Bream also come on the bed in April. Sauger and stripe have headed for deep water by then. Then largemouth bass get the urge and have their business taken care of by the end of June. Catfish spawn late, usually in June. They nest under logs, in holes in the bank, in discarded refrigerators, and in barrels.

By summer the catfishing is good at night, as is angling for crappie and bass. Most species move into the shallow areas to sample forage fish and crayfish after dark.

When fall comes and the water cools, bass begin to move into the shallows to feed on the large schools of shad.

Wintertime angling is most productive in the deep channel drop-offs and ledges and the pockets in the mouth of the river. You can expect to catch sauger, stripe, and crappie at the mouth from November until March.

From near the Williamson–Davidson county line downstream, the Harpeth's fishing gets better, but it is underused. Bank fishing is available in many places near bridges and where a road runs close to it. Ask permission when you want to fish on private property, and be respectful of the land so you and others can return.

FACILITIES

Canoe Rental
   Tip-a-Canoe. Route 2, Box 114, Kingston Springs, TN 37082 (615-254-0836 and 797-2674).

CHAPTER TWENTY-TWO

STONES RIVER

THE EAST AND WEST FORKS OF THE STONES River join to form the headwaters of Percy Priest Lake. The area where they merge is simply called the forks. Beginning in January, it is an especially good place to fish with live bait for rockfish. Stripe kick off their pre-spring feeding run to the forks in February, the same month crappie fishing along the deep drop-offs quickens. Bass angling attains an excellent rating in March. All these species maintain a very-good-to-excellent fishing classification into May.

These headwater streams have good fishing beyond Priest Lake. Drifting in a canoe is the perfect way to fish various stretches of the Stones River system.

THE MIDDLE FORK

The short middle fork runs parallel to I-24 to join the west fork west at the I-24 and US 231 junction. Its headwaters are north of I-24 and Hoovers Gap Road above the Rutherford–Bedford county line. There is a nice, five-mile fish-and-float trip from Elam Road to the US 231 Bridge.

It's another two miles to the TN 99 Bridge, but you will have to negotiate three dams. Below the second dam you will join the flow of the west fork. The last of the three dams is near the TN 99 Bridge.

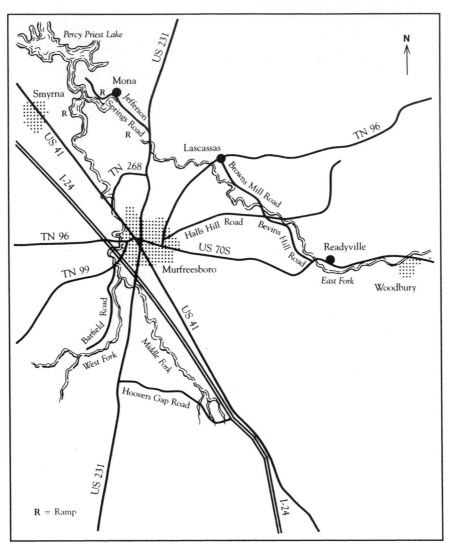

Map Twenty: Stones River Area

Bream, rock bass, and smallies are the primary gamefish in this section. The middle fork is sixteen miles long and shallow with an average depth of about two feet. That's deep enough for a canoe and for fish.

THE WEST FORK

The west fork is twenty-eight miles long, with its headwaters near Rock Springs; it runs parallel to US 231. It takes spring rains to make the upper section navigable. When there is high water, you can put in below the junction of Dry Fork Creek and the west fork at the Walnut Grove Bridge. Panther and Lytle creeks add more volume to the west fork. By the time you reach the middle fork juncture, there is plenty of water.

There are many dams across the west fork. Some are easy to portage, and the one at Manson Pike in east Murfreesboro is considered very dangerous. Put-ins and take-outs are at the bridges beginning at Walnut Grove Road. Going downstream the accesses are Stones River Road, Crescent Road, Barfield Road, TN 99, TN 96, Manson Pike, several bridges in the city of Murfreesboro, US 41, TN 268, Sulphur Springs Road at Nices Mill Dam and Recreation Area, and the West Fork Recreation Area, which is the last take-out point before the west fork joins the east fork. You will experience a lack of flow at Nices Mill because you are entering Priest Lake.

The same fish species swim in the west fork as in the middle fork with the addition of crappie, rockfish, stripe, hybrids, largemouth bass, Kentucky bass, and—rarely—walleye. These species make their way from Priest Lake upstream. I wouldn't consider all these species abundant. Crappie, stripe, rockfish, and hybrids are more plentiful in early spring.

THE EAST FORK

The east fork is twenty-nine miles long. It is better suited for travel and has better fishing. It contains largemouth bass, smallmouth bass, crappie, rock bass, bream, rockfish, stripe, hybrids, and walleye.

The east fork's headwaters are east of Woodbury. Put in at Hollis Creek Road and float ten miles down to Readyville Mill. It's about four miles to Halls Hill Road Bridge, another four miles to Browns Mill Road in the community of Halls Hill, and another four miles to Guy James Road. It is Guy James Road to the locals, although maps have it as Guy Jones Road. From Guy James Road it is a little over 1.5 miles to Browns Mill and Dam. The old mill is an impressive site, and there is good fishing below the dam. From the dam it is 3.5 miles to TN 96 Bridge in Lascassas, about four miles to Betty Ford Road, and about five more miles to US 231 and Walter Hill Dam. Walter Hill Dam is a popular summertime swimming hole known for its smallmouth bass. It is six miles to the USACE Mona Recreation Area on Priest Lake and, finally, the last take-out before the meeting of the forks, East Fork Recreation Area about three miles below Mona.

Doss Neal is an ardent stream fisherman who has spent many hours wading these forks and feeder creeks. He uses two- and four-pound test line to cast one thirty-second and one-sixteenth-ounce jigs on a five-foot ultralight rod. Small plastic crawfish dress his jigs and prove to be the best lure under most fishing conditions. Small Floating Rapalas and Rooster Tail spinners make up a well-rounded selection. Doss says he doesn't like to carry a lot of gear when wading, so he carries a few of the baits necessary to cover various fishing conditions. Shallow water, fast water, root tangles, undercut banks, and deep pools are typical conditions.

Doss catches smallmouth bass, rock bass, and bream. As most stream fishermen, he fishes for two-pound smallies. They give the best fight of the stream fish. They don't get much larger in small streams.

When Doss and I canoed from Guy James Road to Lascassas one spring, the current was too swift for fishing during the first part of our trip. We were moving and casting at structure we didn't have time to fish properly. Carp were the only takers we had until we fished below Browns Mill Dam. The water was not fast below the dam due to the large pool. This is a popular fishing spot.

The stretch of river near Lascassas was slower and deeper. Bradley Creek joins the east fork just above the TN 96 Bridge. We paddled up Bradley Creek to do our best fishing of the trip, catching rock bass, bream, and smallies. Fishing the mouth of Bradley was good too. In fact, our best fishing was within walking distance of our take-out spot at the bridge.

Historic Browns Mill and Dam on the East Fork of the Stones River is one of eleven dams canoeists must negotiate.

Stream anglers are secretive about their fishing holes because most streams will not withstand a lot of fishing pressure. With maps of Cannon and Rutherford counties, you can see the many tributaries to the three forks. (Write or call the county's chamber of commerce for maps, or contact one of the state agencies. *See Appendix A.*)

Mike Kelton of Murfreesboro told me about catching five-pound smallies from the east fork while he was fishing with maggots on the bottom. His friend Mike Nipper grew these little larvae and said he could get them to take up color so that you can choose red, green, white, or blue larvae. Since that conversation, I have seen several magazines advertising maggots. They seem to be catching on as a good fish bait, but I have not tried them yet.

Because there are eleven dams on the three forks of the Stones River and sometimes wire across the streams, be alert for these and other hazards. Swift water at the dams can sweep you into situations you would rather avoid. Bank your craft and scout ahead for portage sites and safe routes. Once you are below the dams, you will usually find excellent fishing.

Drifting down any of these forks, you are likely to see a great deal of wildlife along the banks, from deer and raccoons to waterbirds. Cathy, my wife, used to solo the east fork photographing wildlife. Her fondest memory of canoeing the east fork is of seeing a great horned owl.

You can spend many enjoyable hours cruising down these scenic streams. A lot of Tennessee's history was made on this river system, from the Battle of Stones River during the Civil War to the homes of President Andrew Jackson and John Donelson and the Two Rivers Mansion built by David McGavock, all located close to the Stones River. Early commerce flourished along the Stones River as witnessed by the many small dams and mills that still remain along the three forks. Even if you don't go fishing, Browns Mill and Readyville Mill are worth a trip.

CHAPTER TWENTY-THREE

THE BUFFALO RIVER

THE BUFFALO RIVER ORIGINATES IN LAWRENCE County east of the community of Henryville, Tennessee. It terminates 120 miles later when it joins the Duck River just before emptying into the Tennessee River east of New Johnsonville, Tennessee.

It is a scenic Class I-II stream. Beware of "strainers," trees that have fallen across the river. They can be a nuisance and even deadly if you get swept into one and become trapped. They are most dangerous during high water.

The first put-in is at the Henryville Bridge on TN 240 with the last take-out at Martin Ford 109 miles later. Lewis County has five bridge crossings; Wayne County has four; Perry County has fourteen; and Humphreys County has three. Most of these access points are at bridges, and ease of access varies from fair to good.

ACCESS POINTS

Henryville Bridge
River-mile 117.0. The bridge is one mile east of Henryville on TN 240 on the east side of the river and north side of the highway. *Gamefish Species:* largemouth and smallmouth bass, rock bass, and bream. Rated as *Fair Fishing.*

Barnsville Bridge
River-mile 112.0. Two miles west of the community of Barnsville on Railroad Pike is a washed low-water bridge. Launching from the bank may be more to your liking. *Gamefish Species:* as above. Rated as *Good Fishing.*

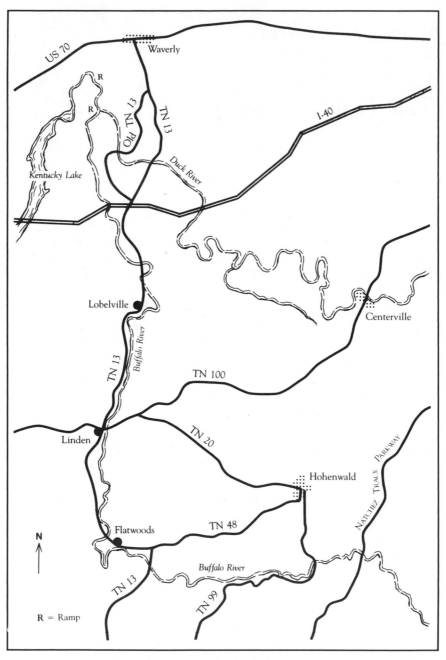

Map Twenty-one: The Buffalo River Area

Natchez Trace Parkway at Metal Ford
River-mile 102.0. This historic site is the first exit off the parkway past the Buffalo River if you are going south. If you are going north, it is four miles north of the Lawrence–Lewis county line. There is about a fifty-yard portage from the parking lot to the river. *Gamefish Species:* as above. Rated as *Good Fishing.*

Grinders Creek Bridge
River-mile 98.2. A new bridge on TN 99, 4.5 miles east of Riverside near the community of Oak Grove. This is an excellent access point. *Gamefish Species:* as above. Fishing is getting better because there is more water. There are trout in the Little Buffalo River, which is downstream on the south side of the Buffalo. Rated as *Good Fishing.*

Texas Bottom Bridge
River-mile 93.5. Located 0.5 miles east of Riverside. *Gamefish Species:* as above. Rated as *Good Fishing* and getting better.

Riverside
River-mile 90.7. Access in the community of Riverside downstream from the bridge. *Gamefish Species:* as above. Rated as *Good Fishing,* almost excellent.

Topsy Bridge
River-mile 80.4. Fair access on the north side of the bridge. Upstream from the bridge a few tenths of a mile is Forty-Eight Creek. There is an access point on the south side of the Buffalo a short way downstream from the creek mouth. *Gamefish Species:* as above with the addition of catfish and trout. The trout are in Forty-Eight Creek. Rated as *Excellent Fishing.*

Big Possum Creek Road Bridge
River-mile 74.8. From the junction of TN 13 and TN 48, take the first turn east and continue for two miles until you come to the bridge. Access is on east side of road and north side of the river. *Gamefish Species:* as above. Rated as *Excellent Fishing.* Trout are in Moccasin Creek, the first creek on the south side of the river upstream from the bridge, and in the Green River on the south side of the Buffalo downstream from the bridge.

Bell Bridge
River-mile 73.1. Located on TN 13 with easy access on south side of river. There are two campgrounds on the north side (*see* camping section below). *Gamefish Species:* Crappie have joined the list with bass, catfish, bream, rock bass, and trout. Big blue catfish live in the deep holes. Mrs.

Ruth Kennamer of Buffalo Shoals told me a friend of hers caught a blue cat weighing eighty-seven pounds and two smaller ones weighing over fifty pounds each. Rated as *Excellent Fishing.*

Slink Shoal
River-mile 62.9. Southwest from the community of Flatwoods 1.5 miles on asphalt road to Slink Shoal Campgrounds. *Gamefish Species:* as above. Rated as *Excellent Fishing.*

Flatwoods Bridge
River-mile 59.1. Access at Little Possum Creek, 0.5 miles south of Flatwoods on TN 13, turn east, and go until you cross a small creek. The access is down a steep road on a gravel bar on the south side of the river. There are two canoe rental businesses in Flatwoods (*see* below). *Gamefish Species:* as above. Rated as *Excellent Fishing.*

New Sugar Hill Bridge
River-mile 52.2. Access is under the bridge located 2.5 miles east of TN 13 on Sugar Hill Road. *Gamefish Species:* as above. There are trout in Sinking Creek and Hurricane Creek. Sinking Creek is the first creek upstream from the bridge and can be accessed from Sinking Creek Road. Hurricane Creek is downstream from the bridge on the east side and can be accessed from Hurricane Creek Road off Old State Highway 20. Rated as *Excellent Fishing.*

Duncan's Camp
River-mile 45.5. Private property near Bethel; must have permission to enter land. Access on gravel bar on south side of river. *Gamefish Species:* as above. Rated as *Excellent Fishing.*

Short Creek Bridge
River-mile 41.4. Near Linden, 0.5 miles south of US 100 on TN 13, turn east and go 0.25 miles. Access on west side of bridge and north side of river. *Gamefish Species:* as above. Rated as *Excellent Fishing.*

Doug Ford
River-mile 27.0. South of Lobelville 1.2 miles, turn off TN 13 on a farm road in the bend of the highway and follow it to the river. Access is a gravel bar. Between Short Creek and Doug Ford are two trout streams that enter from the east. Brush Creek is about six miles downstream of Short Creek, and Cane Creek is a little over three miles farther where TN 50 crosses the Buffalo River. *Gamefish Species:* as above with trout in the streams mentioned. Rated as *Excellent Fishing.*

Linda D'Errico and David Orth stroke their way down one of Tennessee's most popular canoeing streams.

Guiltier Bridge

River-mile 22.7. A half-mile north of Lobelville is a gravel road to the east; follow it for one hundred yards to the pumping station and access to the Buffalo. *Gamefish Species:* as above. Rated as *Excellent Fishing.*

Blue Hole Ridge

River-mile 13.0. One mile south of I-40, turn west off TN 13 on Squeeze Bottom Road and go to the bridge. Access is on the north side of the bridge on a gravel bar. *Gamefish Species:* as above. Rated as *Excellent Fishing.*

Martin Ford

River-mile 8.1. Private property; permission required. South of Baker-ville 1.5 miles, turn off Buffalo Road on to Anderson Road. Access is on the west side of the river on a gravel bar. *Gamefish Species:* as above. Rated as *Excellent Fishing.*

Buzzard Cove

This access is on the west bank of the Duck River about three miles downstream from the Buffalo–Duck junction. West of Waverly, go south on Bankrolled Road (watch for a 90-degree westerly turn—if you go straight, you are on Forks River Road); then take Buzzard Cove Road to the east (second left after crossing the Duck River). *Gamefish Species:* as above with the addition of sauger, walleye, stripe bass, spotted bass, and brassy bass. Rated as *Excellent Fishing.*

FACILITIES

Canoe Rentals and Campgrounds

Crazy Horse Recreation Park, Route 3, Box 199, Waynesboro, TN 38485 (615-722-5213). RV, primitive camping, swimming, picnicking, bath houses, restaurant, arts/dance pavillion (1,500 capacity), fishing, canoe trips from a few hours to weeks. Jerry West will put you in and take you out at the places you request. Caters to large groups.

Buffalo Shoals, Route 3, Box 201, Waynesboro, TN 38485 (615-722-3960). Campsites, swimming, fishing, picnicking, canoe trips of any length. Thomas and Ruth Kennamer operate a small grocery store with some fishing and picnic supplies.

Flatwoods Canoe Base, Route 4, Box 612B, Flatwoods, TN 37096 (615-589-5661). Camping, fishing, swimming, canoe trips of any length. Small but very accommodating; make arrangements to suit your time frame at no extra charge. Air boat rides available.

Buffalo River Canoe Rental Co., Route 4, Box 510, Flatwoods, TN 37096 (615-589-2755 or 589-5403). Camping, swimming, fishing, picnicking, canoeing. Special trips arranged; caters to large groups.

Heath's Canoe Rental, Lobelville, TN 37097 (615-593-2306 or 589-2345). Fishing/picnic supplies, limited-range canoe trips. Call for info and reservations.

Clearwater Canoe Company, PO Box 321, Waynesboro, TN 38485 (615-722-3081). Campgrounds, canoes.

PART FOUR

CRAPPIE FISHING

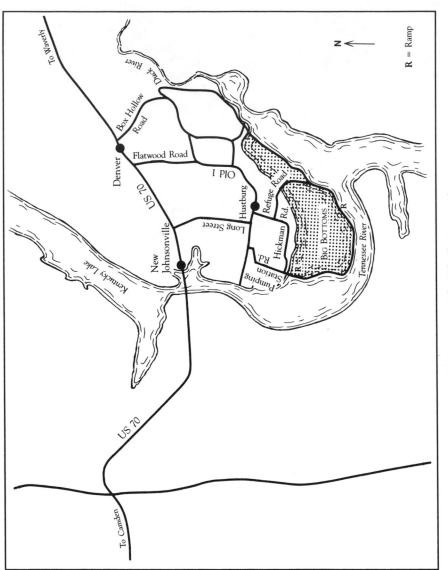

Map Twenty-two: The Big Bottoms Area

CHAPTER TWENTY-FOUR

BIG BOTTOMS

THIS CHAPTER IS ESPECIALLY FOR CRAPPIE anglers. The area called Big Bottoms was once the largest cornfield in the world. Forty-three thousand acres of rich bottom land were cultivated until the TVA bought it for flood control in 1945 and it became part of Kentucky Lake.

"The TVA made the levee to control the direction of the river's flow and to reduce the mosquito population," says Mark Musaus, assistant refuge manager in Paris, Tennessee. The U.S. Fish and Wildlife Service began developing the area as a wildlife refuge in 1945. "We encourage the public to come and appreciate the refuge's wildlife." That includes crappie.

The Big Bottoms is in Humphreys County. About fifteen miles west of Waverly at the junction of US 70 and the Tennessee River is the community of New Johnsonville. Just a few miles south of New Johnsonville is the Duck River unit of the Tennessee National Wildlife Refuge. This is the Big Bottoms area.

Parts of Big Bottoms were flooded to make nine lakes with stumps and cypress trees in the shallow impoundments. At low water you can see the thousands of stumps and logs. During times of high water, which rises with the river, the stump tops are just below the surface.

Since the water is shallow, it warms rapidly in the spring sunshine. When the water temperature reaches the 62- to 65-degree range, you can depend on reproductive urges activating the crappie.

Under normal warming conditions, the water is just right by the end of April and full tilt in May.

If the weather throws a cold front, however, the crappie are less likely to respond to your bait just as they would be on any other water. With patience—that is, keeping a lively minnow around a stump longer than on good days—you can still share in the secret of Big Bottoms.

"The secret is size. You can catch lots of crappie on the river, but the ones you catch here are going to be a lot bigger," says T. C. Bailey, a local angler. The "here" Mr. Bailey refers to is the 1,210-acre New Johnsonville Pumping Station Impoundment located near the western edge of the Tennessee National Migratory Wildlife Refuge.

"That's the secret of this place. You may catch an ice chest full on the river, but from here it only takes half as many crappie to fill a chest." Bailey lives nearby and frequently fishes the pumping station reservoir. He uses a john boat with a fifteen-horsepower motor and a trolling motor for maneuvering among the stumps. He rarely catches crappie less than one-half pound and usually has several that are close to two pounds.

"Most people just want to catch a lot—size doesn't matter to them. But now that the limit is thirty per day, size makes a difference to me." Crappie have a tasty white meat that is great when fried or blackened. Bailey says crappie is the only fish he eats.

There is another secret besides big crappie. It's never crowded. Bailey says most anglers fish the pumping station water in the spring, and on a crowded day you can count all the boats on the fingers of three hands.

There is a rare peacefulness here for anglers to appreciate. Some days you can have the whole place to yourself and see the sun rise while watching ducks, herons, and bitterns starting their day or a deer drinking at the water's edge. Enjoy listening to nature's sounds, but when you hear the splashing of fish chasing their breakfast, you will quickly get primed for some serious crappie fishing.

My wife and I made our first trip to the pumping station years ago on a calm May day. We were less than fifty yards from the launch when Cathy caught a crappie. It was the first one I had ever seen that weighed more than two pounds, and this was her first time crappie fishing. She had just plopped her minnow down by a stump and bingo! It was quite a fight on a fly rod. We soon caught a few more and had enough for several dinners, proving what Mr. Bailey

A fly rod rigged for minnow fishing is ideal for angling among the many stumps in Big Bottoms.

said: "The secret is size."

John Conder, fish biologist of Tennessee Wildlife Resources Agency, speculates about the reasons crappie are larger here than in the main river: "It has excellent conditions for crappie because it stays clear in the spring. If you look at it from the air, you can see the Duck and Tennessee rivers running muddy. Fish conditions are more ideal here than in Kentucky Lake.

"When the water temperature reaches 50–54 degrees, crappie start their pre-spawn move. By May they are well into spawning. They select a place just below light penetration on some sort of structure," says Conder.

Bank anglers can walk along the rock levee and cast into the most productive waters in the reservoir. Conder says he thinks the best fishing is near the pumping station. The station has walkways on two sides offering access to the deepest part of the impoundment in front of the pump house.

The refuge closes to boats on the first of November, or whenever the migratory birds arrive, and reopens in mid-March when the birds leave. This is a sanctuary for wintering waterfowl and other birds, including raptors. The impoundment is open to bank fishing year-round. When it is open to boats, some areas may be closed to boat traffic because of nesting eagles and ospreys. These restricted areas don't include the best fishing spots that are south of the launch site.

Since the bottom is rather uniform throughout the impoundment, except for creek channels, you will find spawning black crappie mixed in with the white. In general, white crappie spawn in

Local angler T. C. Bailey is a regular customer for Big Bottoms' crappie.

slightly shallower areas, and they don't mind a mud bottom or murky water. The black crappie prefer clearer water, a hard bottom, and spawn in water deeper than the white.

Both crappie have black spots. The black crappie's spots are numerous and without a pattern, whereas the white crappie has fewer spots arranged in a vague vertical pattern. You probably won't need to know the difference unless you face the happy encounter of a record fish. The only comments I have heard about the two cousins at the pumping station is that there seem to be more white crappie than black, which is usually the case in the South. Sometimes they will mate and have hybrid offspring. But how would you know?

If you catch a black crappie that weighs more than 4 pounds, 8 ounces or a white crappie over 5 pounds, 3 ounces, you will have the new world record. The record fish came from Virginia and Mississippi, respectively. The next record also should come from the South, maybe from the pumping station impoundment.

"This place is one giant stakebed," claims Doss Neal of Nashville. He says it reminds him of Reelfoot Lake. "This place has everything Reelfoot Lake has except the number of fishermen. I also like it because the crappie I catch are bigger." Neal says that when he fishes here, the smallest crappie on his stringer are three-quarters of a pound, with the largest running two pounds. "We suspend a minnow about a foot down from the float and drop it by stump after stump. We're constantly moving. It's not uncommon for two of us to put our bait by one stump and pull out two crappie."

There are two deep channels that lead away from the launch, one to the east and the other to the south. There are many islands sprinkled throughout the impoundment; some aren't much larger than a bassboat, and others are an acre or more. This makes a lot of shoreline to fish, and some of it is laced with weed beds.

There are no guides for the impoundment. Talking to other anglers like Neal or Bailey is the best way to learn the water. During May there is probably a crappie at every stump and tree, so you don't need a guide. But if you wait later than May, you will have to fish harder to locate the slabs.

The most popular method for catching these slabs is using a ten-foot crappie pole or a fly rod with a minnow about eight inches below a bobber. The minnow is lifted and plunked down next to a stump. If there are no takers in a short time, usually ten to fifteen seconds, anglers turn on their trolling motors and continue weaving among the stick-ups.

A one-sixteenth-ounce jig with a plastic curlytail under a bobber is another excellent method to entice crappie. Different anglers
swear by different colors and styles. My impression is that just about
anything will work if you put it in front of the fish. The jig and
bobber method is very effective, especially if there is any wind. The
wave action will make your jig dance. In calmer water, cast beyond a
stump and work your bait back slowly with sharp jerks to make the
curlytail wiggle.

A new generation of plastic baits has arrived, with scents and
flavors incorporated into their matrix. I'm not talking about salt and
sugar, which have been around for many years. The active ingre-
dients are amino acids, amines, and amides. Dr. Keith Jones, direc-
tor of research at Berkley, spent years isolating compounds that
influence a fish's eating behavior in a positive way. These baits are
available in Berkley's line of Power Baits, and some are specifically
made for crappie.

Berkley isn't the only company employing these scents and
flavors. You can find many others who do. Mister Twister has added
a new twist to the scent line of baits: bananas. Their tests showed
fish like that flavor. Harold Morgan, a crappie guide from Nashville,
says he knows a guide on Kentucky Lake that cuts open cantaloupes
and sinks them to attract crappie.

If you elect to use the minnow and bobber technique, use
a thin wire hook and twelve-pound test line. The hook will
straighten before the line breaks and save you the time and labor of
retying. You can heat your jig hook with a match or lighter to
remove some of its temper. This allows the hook to bend, and it can
be yanked off that inevitable snag.

Crappie are not known for furious hits and runs—they hit with
finesse. But you can usually tell when a crappie bites. Your bobber
will descend slowly and steadily. When you are using minnows,
don't use less than a number 8 hook. Small hooks can tear through
the thin lip membranes. Larger hooks are more likely to hold the
fish, and crappie have large mouths to accommodate these hooks.

Anglers have varying opinions about what lure works best. For
instance, jig anglers have favorite dressings they tie or slide over the
hook. Some like the white marabou; others prefer a small spinner
blade combination, and so on. I talked to a couple of young men
who had the beginnings of a good string of crappie, but not a limit.
They were leaving because they had lost all their blue-skirted jigs.

Nashville's Harold Morgan is the king of Priest Lake crappie fishing.

They didn't have confidence anything else would catch fish and said they had tried other colors. Meanwhile, my wife and I kept catching fish with our white curlytails—needless to say, we didn't believe in the blue-jig-skirt theory. Often it's the angler's attitude that makes the difference.

You can sometimes double your crappie action by using the safety-pin-shaped wire from small spinner baits rigged with a jig on the bottom and a number 1 hook in a curlytail grub placed on the top wire. This gives a new meaning to "double your pleasure." This rig works well on crappie and on schooling fish. It is very challenging when used on ultralight gear.

Sometimes you may want to anchor to fish an area thoroughly. My wife and I use this method to explore the many stick-ups. We use a canoe because it is maneuverable and requires only a lightweight anchor fore and aft to hold our position.

Due to the abundance of stumps and trees, canoes and john boats are the best choices for this water. Plenty of anglers use bass boats; but some places are not easily accessible, and maneuvering these big boats can be a chore.

Although crappie are the main attraction at the pumping station impoundment, plenty of bass are caught here. They are usually a bonus to crappie anglers. This water is rich in fish other than crappie and bass, including catfish, stripe, bream, gar, and even sauger.

DIRECTIONS

To get to the pumping station, turn south off Highway 70 in New Johnsonville on to Long Street. Continue to the stop sign and turn right. Turn left 0.7 miles later, then bear to the right when the road forks. Just over the rise is the Tennessee River, and the pumping station launch is left of the parking lot.

To get to the other lakes in Big Bottoms, turn left at the end of Long Street, turn right before you get to Hustburg Store, go a little over 0.5 miles, and turn left. The paved road ends when you enter the refuge. From the gravel roads you can reach the other lakes. The bigger ones are on your left as you enter the refuge. These lakes are not on a map, so look for the signs.

FACILITIES

Accommodations

The community of New Johnsonville is on the east side of the Tennessee River Bridge on US 70. There you can find restaurants (like Cove Hollow, which features a catfish buffet), campgrounds, and a baitshop.

Anchor Inn Campground, Marina & Resort, PO Box J, Highway 70, New Johnsonville, TN 37134 (615-535-2897). Write or call about campgrounds and other facilities near motel.

Baitshops or Fishing Supplies

TJ's Baitshop, Tony and Judy King, Highway 70W, New Johnsonville, TN 37134 (615-535-3258). They can tell you where the action is and how to get in on it. Next to Anchor Inn Motel at foot of bridge.

Dreaden's Baitshop, on US 70, east side of Waverly (615-269-1998). Full line of fishing supplies, deli. Donnie Dreaden can tell you where the fish are biting.

For more information about Big Bottoms and the refuge, call the U.S. Fish and Wildlife Service (901-642-2091) or write the U.S. Department of the Interior, U.S. Fish and Wildlife Service, PO Box 849, Paris, TN 38242.

CONCLUSION

I hope you found many helpful tips and enough solid information in this book with details to help you find and catch more fish. Data about fishing and fish behavior are growing rapidly, and you can improve your fishing by reading books and magazines. Appendix E lists some good publications for you to consider.

I strongly recommend the *Tennessee Sportsman* magazine because the editor, Bill Hartlage, presents state-specific information about our waters, our gamefish, and new techniques that anglers, like yourself, have developed.

Keep up with changes in Tennessee's fishing laws by reading the TWRA's *Fishing Regulations*. This little pamphlet should be available where you purchase yor license.

Please use caution and be aware of dangers. You can avoid harm by being alert to potential hazards. As Jimmy Holt, the host of "The Tennessee Outdoorsmen," is always reminding us, "Be sure to wear your life jacket."

While I made every reasonable effort to be accurate, I'm sure I have missed some important places, techniques, and even a road sign or two. Please send me your comments, suggestions, or corrections. I am interested in presenting the most reliable and comprehensive information available. Thank you, and I hope you have great fishing!

Vernon Summerlin
5550 Boy Scout Rd.
Franklin, TN 37064-9565

David Woodward of Nashville unhooks a yellow curlytail jig from a Lake Barkley crappie.

APPENDIXES

APPENDIX A

Maps, Accommodations and Other Information

TVA MAPS AND SURVEY DEPARTMENT
100 Haney Building
Chattanooga, TN 37041
615-751-MAPS
    751-6277

Write or call for catalog of maps. Anglers would be interested in navigational charts, navigation-recreation maps, boat docks, topographic maps, and underwater contour maps.

DEPARTMENT OF CONSERVATION
Tennessee Division of Geology
Map Sales Publication Office
701 Broadway
Nashville, TN 37243-0445
615-742-6706

Catalog contains maps and books on streams. As anglers, you will be interested in topographical maps of Tennessee's lakes and geologic quadrangle maps.

U.S. ARMY CORPS OF
    ENGINEERS
Public Affairs Office
PO Box 1070
Nashville, TN 37202-1070
615-736-7161

USACE
Natural Resources Management
    Branch
PO Box 1070
Nashville, TN 37202-1070
615-736-5115

USACE offers excellent maps of its lakes, and some are free for the asking. Maps include launching ramps, marinas, campgrounds, recreation areas, and other information useful to the angler—or anyone seeking outdoor facilities and fun. These are *must get* maps. You can receive a weekly fishing report by asking Public Affairs to put you on their mailing list.

U.S. ARMY CORPS OF ENGINEERS
Map Section
PO Box 1070
Nashville, TN 37202-1070
615-736-5641

Topographical maps of the lakes. They come in many sheets, 11" × 17" or larger, giving details of structure to look for with your LCG. Anglers should have a set of these maps for USACE lakes. They range from $3.75 to $12.00. Each USACE lake chapter has its resource manager's name, address, and phone number listed.

TENNESSEE WILDLIFE RESOURCES AGENCY
PO Box 40747
Nashville, TN 37204
615-781-6622

Lake maps with locations of fish attractors.

DELORME MAPPING CO.
PO Box 298
Freeport, Maine 04032
207-865-4171

A book of maps detailing all of Tennessee and many other states: back roads to our fishing holes, boat ramps, and campgrounds. In bookstores for $12.95.

KENTUCKY DEPT. OF FISH AND WILDLIFE RESOURCES
State Office Building Annex
Frankfort, KY 40601

TENNESSEE TOURIST DEVELOPMENT
PO Box 23170
Nashville, TN 37202
615-741-2158

Diverse information about fishing, accommodations, and camping and many other useful brochures and maps.

KENTUCKY LAKE VACATIONLAND
Route 7, Box 145
Benton, KY 42025
502-527-7665

and

TENNESSEE'S KENTUCKY LAKE ASSOCIATION
PO Box 428
Paris, TN 38242
901-232-8211

Information about fishing Lake Barkley and the Land Between the Lakes.

The following phone numbers are for dam generation schedules, lake elevations, and fishing conditions. All are area code 615 except Lake Barkley.

Dam Generation Schedules
1 • Dale Hollow   243-3408
2 • Cordell Hull   735-9320
3 • Center Hill   548-8581 or 858-4366
4 • Old Hickory   824-7766
5 • Priest   883-2351
6 • Cheatham   792-5697 or 254-3734
7 • Barkley   502-362-8430
8 • Others   736-5455

APPENDIX B

CHAMBERS OF COMMERCE

Cheatham County Chamber of
Commerce
PO Box 354
Ashland City, TN 37015
615-792-6722

Clarksville Area Chamber of
Commerce
PO Box 883
Clarksville, TN 37041
615-626-4149

Columbia–Maury County
Chamber of Commerce
PO Box 1076
Columbia, TN 38402
615-388-2155

Cookeville–Putnam County
Chamber of Commerce
302 South Jefferson
Cookeville, TN 38501
615-526-2211

Crossville–Cumberland County
Chamber of Commerce
108 South Main
Crossville, TN 38555
615-484-8444

Dale Hollow–Clay County
Chamber of Commerce
PO Box 69
Celina, TN 38551
615-243-3338

Dickson County Chamber of
Commerce
PO Box 339
Dickson, TN 37055
615-446-2349

Donelson–Hermitage Chamber
of Commerce
3051 Lebanon Road
Nashville, TN 37214
615-883-7896

Dover–Stewart County
    Chamber of Commerce
PO Box 147
Dover, TN 37058
615-232-8290

Fayetteville–Lincoln County
    Chamber of Commerce
PO Box 515
Fayetteville, TN 37334
615-433-1234

Franklin County Chamber of
    Commerce
PO Box 280
Winchester, TN 37398
615-967-6788

Gallatin Chamber of
    Commerce
PO Box 26
Gallatin, TN 37066
615-452-4000

Giles County Chamber of
    Commerce
203 South First Street
Pulaski, TN 38478
615-363-3789

Goodlettsville Chamber of
    Commerce
405 Two Mile Parkway
Goodlettsville, TN 37072
615-859-1384

Grundy County Chamber of
    Commerce
HCR 76, Box 578
Gruetli-Lager, TN 37339
615-779-3462

Hendersonville Chamber of
    Commerce
101 Wessington Place
Hendersonville, TN 37075
615-824-2818

Hohenwald Chamber of
    Commerce
PO Box 182
Hohenwald, TN 38462
615-796-4084

Humphreys County Chamber of
    Commerce
PO Box 733
Waverly, TN 37185
615-296-4865

Jamestown–Fentress County
    Chamber of Commerce
PO Box 1904
Jamestown, TN 38556
615-879-9948

Lebanon–Wilson County
    Chamber of Commerce
149 Public Square
Lebanon, TN 37087
615-444-5503

Livingston–Overton County
    Chamber of Commerce
PO Box 354
Livingston, TN 38570
615-823-6421

Lynchburg–Moore County
    Chamber of Commerce
Box 345
Lynchburg, TN 37352
615-759-4655

Madison Chamber of
Commerce
PO Box 97
Madison, TN 37207
615-865-5400

Manchester Chamber of
Commerce
110 East Main Street
Manchester, TN 37355
615-728-7635

McMinnville–Warren County
Chamber of Commerce
PO Box 574
McMinnville, TN 37110
615-473-6611

Mt. Juliet–West Wilson
County Chamber of
Commerce
PO Box 487
Mt. Juliet, TN 37122
615-758-3478

Nashville Area Chamber of
Commerce
161 Fourth Avenue North
Nashville, TN 37219
615-259-3900

Rutherford County Chamber of
Commerce
302 South Front Street
Murfreesboro, TN 37133
615-893-6565

Shelbyville–Bedford County
Chamber of Commerce
100 North Cannon Boulevard
Shelbyville, TN 37160
615-684-3482

Smith County Chamber of
Commerce
PO Box 70
Carthage, TN 37030
615-735-2093

Smithville–Dekalb County
Chamber of Commerce
PO Box 64
Smithville, TN 37166
615-597-4263

Sparta–White County
Chamber of Commerce
16 West Bockman
Sparta, TN 38583
615-836-3552

Springfield–Robertson County
Chamber of Commerce
100 Fifth Avenue West
Springfield, TN 37172
615-384-3800

Tullahoma Chamber of
Commerce
PO Box 1205
Tullahoma, TN 37388
615-455-5497

Wayne County Chamber of
Commerce
PO Box 675
Waynesboro, TN 37388
615-722-3952

Williamson County Chamber
of Commerce
PO Box 156
Franklin, TN 37065
615-794-1225

FISHING GUIDES OF MIDDLE TENNESSEE

South Harpeth Outfitters
PO Box 218226
Nashville, TN 37221
615-646-5875

Mike Sanderlin and Ernie Paquette specialize in stream fishing with fly and spinning gear. They provide everything from transportation to a gourmet lunch.

Harold Morgan
1311 Cardinal Drive
Nashville, TN 37216
615-227-9337

Harold has specialized in crappie fishing for twenty-one years. He guides on Priest and Old Hickory. He will also take you fishing for bass and rockfish.

Corporate Guide Service
Gene Austin
2825 Twin Lawn Drive
Nashville, TN 37214
615-871-4109

Corporate Guide Service has ten guides with specialties in all species of fish and on almost all the lakes in Middle Tennessee. Guide Gene Austin is a two-time state fishing champion and holds the state's lake trout record.

Tony Bean's Fishing Guides
Elm Hill Marina
1240 Pleasant Hill Road
Nashville, TN 37217
615-889-5363

Tony is an expert smallmouth angler. His guides are

Dayton Blair for largemouth and smallmouth bass, crappie, hybrids, and stripers on Priest and Old Hickory. Richard Craig guides for hybrids, stripers, largemouth, and smallmouth bass on Priest.

Jim McClain
Route 5, Box 5310
Winchester, TN 37398
615-967-3631

Jim has all the techniques and equipment you need for catching rockfish. His boat is "armed and dangerous" when it comes to locating and downrigging for the big fish.

Ed Garner
Contact Ed at Morris Ferry Dock on Woods Reservoir
Route 2, Box 144
Estill Springs, TN 37330
615-967-5370

Clyde Hill, Jr.
Route 2, Box 503
Estill Springs, TN 37330
615-967-6463

Clyde specializes in fishing Woods Reservoir.

Jack Christian
132 Peggy Court
Goodlettsville, TN 37072
615-672-0194

Jack is a smallmouth specialist on Priest. He guides for largemouth, hybrids, and stripers on Priest and Old Hickory. He says April is his hottest smallmouth month, and his clients boat between fifty and seventy-five fish. He says five or more will be big smallmouth.

Betty and Johnny Riddle
Route 4
Tims Ford State Park
Winchester, TN 37398
615-967-9668

Betty and Johnny operate the marina/restaurant in Tims Ford Park and provide guiding for the lake's many species.

James Blair and
Dayton Blair
1180 Pleasant Grove Road
Mount Juliet, TN 37122
615-754-1256

James and Dayton will take you on Priest and Old Hickory for bass, hybrids, rockfish, and crappie.

Ira Barlow
Route 3, Box 94
Celina, TN 38551
615-243-2743

Ira guides out of Cedar Hill Resort on Dale Hollow Lake.

Ralph Dallas
668 Happy Hollow Road
Goodlettsville, TN 37072
615-824-5792

Ralph specializes in trophy stripers on Old Hickory, Norris, and Lake Cumberland. He is a renowned striper taxidermist.

Ernie Kilpatrick
(N/A)
615-455-9412

Tims Ford and Priest are Ernie's favorite lakes for stripers, smallmouth, and largemouth bass, but he will take you on the Cumberland River and Norris. He provides transportation upon request.

Scott Morris
2221 North Berrys Chapel Road
Franklin, TN 37064
615-794-8708

Scott works Old Hickory and Priest for smallmouth bass and stripers. He can take you stream fishing for smallmouth and pond fishing for largemouth.

Chris Nischan
(N/A)
615-269-3441

Chris is a specialist in "Adventure Travel." Contact him through Bill Clay's Sporting Goods, 208 Franklin Road, Nashville, TN 37204.

Fred McClintock
Route 3, Box 272
Celina, TN 37551
615-243-2142

Fred is often written about as *the* smallmouth guide on Dale Hollow.

Rock Creek Guide Service
(N/A)
615-649-2143

They guide for rockfish on Tims Ford Lake.

John Ed Garrett
805 North Summerfield Drive
Madison, TN 37115
615-868-5350

John Ed guides exclusively for crappie as he has done for the last twenty-five years. He guides on Old Hickory, Kentucky Lake, and Lake Barkley. He says fishing is still in its heyday on Barkley.

Poor Boy's Tackle
1393 West Broad
Cookeville, TN 38501
615-528-5447

They provide striper guide service.

Jeff Hudson
2456 Fairbrook Drive
Nashville, TN 37214
615-883-6580
     331-1800

Priest, Old Hickory, and Tims Ford are where Jeff will take you for stripers.

R. L. Guy
Route 9, Box 332
Sparta, TN 38583
615-935-2459

Cookeville, TN 38502
615-528-5332

    Guy specializes in walleye.

Bob Masters
Livingston Boat Dock
615-823-2381
    823-6666

Mountain Sound Guides
303 South Willow Avenue

TROUT STREAMS OF MIDDLE TENNESSEE

TWRA STOCKS STREAMS OF MIDDLE TENNES-see with rainbow and brown trout. Doug Markham of Region II can provide you with a list of stocking dates. Call 615-781-6622 or 1-800-624-7406. The following are streams stocked in the spring of 1991:

Bedford County: Normandy Tailwater
Clay County: Obey River
DeKalb County: Pine Creek and Sink Creek
Franklin County: Tims Ford Tailwater
Grundy County: Elk River, Collins River
Hickman County: Mill Creek
Houston County: Hurricane Creek
Humphreys County: Tumbling Creek and Hurricane Creek
Jackson County: Flynns Lick Creek
Lawrence County: Little Buffalo River
Overton County: Standing Stone Lake
Perry County: Cane Creek and Hurricane Creek
Putnam County: Calfkiller Creek
Van Buren County: Rocky River, Cane Creek, and Laurel Creek
Warren County: Charles Creek, North Barren Fork Creek,
    Mountain Creek, and Upper Hills Creek

PUBLICATIONS

Tennessee Sportsman, PO Box 714, Marietta, GA 30061-9973. This magazine is dedicated to fishing and hunting in Tennessee.

Tennessee Wildlife, PO Box 40747, Nashville, TN 37204. A beautiful magazine about Tennessee's fish and game and other outdoor activities, with outstanding photography.

The Tennessee Conservationist, 701 Broadway, Nashville, TN 37243-0440. Another beautiful magazine covering subjects from fish to fall colors. This is a worthwhile magazine of conservation, general outdoor topics, and wonderful photography.

Tackle Test, PO Box 2076, Knoxville, IA 50138. *Tackle Test* magazine is the *Consumer Reports* of the fishing industry. It bench tests and field tests fishing tackle and other supplies made for anglers.

Mid South Hunting and Fishing News, 3251 Poplar Avenue, Suite B-125, Memphis, TN 38111. A tabloid format gives hunting and fishing information for Tennessee and other southern states.

Bassin', 15115 South 76th Avenue, Bixby, OK 74008. A magazine covering freshwater fishing with emphasis on black bass.

Crappie, Same address as *Bassin'*. A new magazine dedicated to crappie anglers.

Field & Stream, 2 Park Avenue, New York, NY 10016. One of the top outdoor magazines with a regional section.

North American Fisherman, Suite 260, 12301 Whitewater Drive, Minnetonka, MN 55343. *NAF* covers all forms of fishing.

Outdoor Life, 2 Park Avenue, New York, NY 10016. One of the top outdoor magazines with a regional section.

Southern Outdoors, PO Box 17915, Montgomery, AL 36141. Covers fishing and hunting in the South.

Bass'n Gal, PO Box 13925, Arlington, TX 76013. Sugar Ferris established *Bass'n Gal* especially for women and for women who want to fish professionally.

Fishing Facts, PO Box 609, Menomonee Falls, WI 53052. This magazine specializes in teaching anglers about structure and fish behavior.

Hooked on Fishing, PO Box 682, Cape Girardeau, MO 63702. Dedicated to family fishing with "how-to" articles.

Bassmaster, 1 Bell Road, Montgomery, AL 36117. Exclusively for bass anglers.

In-Fisherman, PO Box 999, Brainerd, MN 56401. Dedicated to publishing studies of fish behavior.

Kentucky, Happy Hunting Ground, Department of Fish and Wildlife, Frankfort, KY 40601. A magazine similar to *Tennessee Wildlife* and the *Tennessee Conservationist* for Kentuckians.

Outdoor Organizations of Middle Tennessee

Harpeth River Coalition, 231 Second Avenue South, Franklin, TN 37064. An environmental group dedicated to the restoration and conservation of the Harpeth River. Their agenda includes passive parks and canoe ramps on public lands bordering the river so more people have access to the river. They meet the first Monday of every other month and have a newsletter.

Tennessee Scenic Rivers Association, PO Box 159041, Nashville, TN 37215. This group is interested in educational activities and in the conservation of Tennessee's waterways. They have a newsletter and meet in Cheekwood's Botanic Hall.

Trout Unlimited, Contact Chris Nischan at Clay's Sporting Goods, 2708 Franklin Road, Nashville, TN 37204 (615-269-3441). They meet the third Wednesday of each month in Cheekwood's Botanic Hall.

Mail Order Fishing Supplies

Bass Pro Shops, 1935 South Campbell, Springfield, MO 65898. An extensive catalog of mail order fishing and hunting supplies and equipment.

Cabela's, 812 Thirteenth Avenue, Sidney, NB 69160. An excellent mail order catalog for anglers and hunters.

INDEX